THE MIRACLE OF
MEDIUMSHIP

The Miracle of
Mediumship

Angela Dunlop

"There is no end to our evolvement and the potential within us. It is only we who limit ourselves with inhibiting beliefs about our spiritual nature and inherent gifts."

From Glyn Edwards, a renowned medium, remembered.

I would like to dedicate this book to my Mum, Bernadette.

Thank you for your support, love and encouragement throughout my career.

Love you!

Acknowledgements

I WOULD LIKE to offer a special thanks to all of the families who kindly allowed their stories to be shared throughout this book. Without your input, this book wouldn't have manifested. Thank you for being a part of the process and giving your account of events. You are the stars of this book.

Thank you, Gabrielle, my beautiful, wise daughter, for all the love and laughter you bring into my life. That gratitude extends to my family Lisa, Teresa, Bernadette and my dad, Tommy, for each of their support with my work.

Thank you Rose, my editor, your insightful and motivating energy has inspired me through-out the journey of this book. You've been a joy to work with from the beginning to the end.

Thank you to the Belfast Spiritualist Church for helping in my early days of training as a medium, I had many wonderful teachers and guides spurring me on, your input and support is forever appreciated.

Finally, I am grateful to Spirit, for believing in

me when I doubted myself, for your unseen support, love and help that is constantly stream-ing to us all.

Table of Contents

CHAPTER ONE

Friends Reunited

LIKE A PREACHER on Sunday, I am standing on a podium in a tightly packed hall, revealing what I believe to be truth. My name is Angela Dunlop and I'm a psychic medium.

It's an unusual career choice; one often greeted with scepticism. "How can you talk to the dead?" disbelievers argue. *Con artists*, *scammers* and *rip-off merchants* are just some of the derogatory labels bandied about.

My role is to deliver messages from loved ones who have passed to Spirit. For a preacher, the message is filtered from sections of the Bible. For a medium, communication is through the soul of the deceased. Sometimes it's in an audience setting; sometimes it's a one-to-one reading. Spirit communicates through me.

The purpose of having this gift is to provide evidence of life after death. I've seen, time and time again, how this power can transform lives.

Nowhere was this more evident than one particular summer evening. The crowd gathered in front of me were mostly women; all waiting to discover what heavenly insight and inspiration would be revealed. In a babbling hall of sixty eager, chatty voices, I noticed only one man in the corner. I'd guess he was late thirties. Propped against the bar, next to a blonde partner, he had the air of being dragged along for the night to keep his missus company.

"Hello, my name is Angela Dunlop and I work as a medium." I gave a brief introduction and explained my job. "I connect to loved ones who have passed to Spirit. I communicate with them, sharing their memories with you. They relay personal details to me to help you know they are still with you. All I ask is that you keep an open mind."

As I began, I closed my eyes for a few seconds and, in my clairvoyance, I could see a man being shot dead. I became aware that he wanted to talk to the only man in the audience. Opening my eyes, I glanced over at that lone male in the corner and smiled.

"Can I work with you, please?" I asked him.

His face reddened immediately as he shuffled

about in his seat uncomfortably, but he agreed. I noticed the beautiful blonde-haired younger lady sitting beside him.

"This is your partner," I remarked, darting a glance at her while he nodded his head. I teased him a little. "You do realise you're the only man here."

Chuckling, he announced, "Yes, she trailed me along. Told me there'd be other fellas here too."

Everyone laughed and it was apparent he was beginning to relax a little.

"I have your friend from Spirit here. He is keen to talk to you. I know he was shot dead by paramilitaries. He's wearing a black leather jacket, blue jeans and a white t-shirt. I hear the name John."

Astonished, he validated that his friend was wearing exactly those clothes at the time of a fatal shooting, and that his name was, indeed, John.

"He was no angel in life!" I exclaimed. "He got involved with the wrong crowd. He was a rebel who felt a sense of duty to protect the community. I'm getting a vibe that he was in and out of jail over the years. Does that make sense?"

"Yes, love, all of it," he now had my full attention.

He was, of course, referring to that period known as The Troubles, when Belfast's city centre had been out of bounds to the public. To venture outside your own territory was to risk getting a bullet in the head. Taxis were too dangerous; paramilitaries would pose as drivers and just by giving them your address, you were giving away your religious background – your tribal allegiance.

As I was sharing, my awareness shifted. I could feel another male friend standing next to me. "There's someone else here," I stated. "It's interesting because there's another friend coming forward. Both of your mates were murdered. This other man is showing me his last memories of standing in a bar. Several men burst in on him, then took him outside. They put him into the boot of a car and drove away. That's the last time anyone saw him alive." I could clairvoyantly see them driving away with this friend. "They took him to a wasteland and shot him."

The young man in the corner was sweating profusely, clearly wondering how so many personal details of these events could be known. "You're scaring the life out of me here!" he exclaimed.

"I'm not finished yet!" I carried on. "The second friend remembers having a wad of notes in his pockets. He lived for the thrill of life – women, drugs, money."

"Yes, my mate Jim was found with a thousand quid in his pocket when he died," he confirmed.

"Neither of your friends believed in the afterlife. They didn't think about it nor did they have any insight into the work I'm doing. They had no need to," I explained.

"However," I went on, "The amazing thing is their message to you. They are both delighted that you've changed your ways; that you're learning to love." I hesitated. "May I ask – are you thinking of getting engaged to your partner?"

A ripple of laughter rang out among the crowd as the pair gazed at each other, the girl's face lighting up with surprise. He blushed again and then admitted that yes, he was thinking of it. The blonde woman smiled profusely, glowing in this new-found revelation.

"Your friends think this woman has helped to settle you down. She's keeping you on the straight and narrow. They want you to stay away from the wrong crowd."

"Your friend Jim is saying that not only did he

hurt strangers, but he hurt those closest to him. He wanted all the power and glory; to be looked up to, but it wasn't worth it. He made a lot of enemies and he can see now the devastation he caused."

"He hurt his partner deeply," I went on, relaying the words that were coming to me. "He remembers cheating and lying to her, being with other women. I feel he had a child with her and couldn't be there for them. He is sorry for that. He knows he ran away from responsibilities. He is truly helping you in Spirit to be a better man and to be good to the people you love."

"Strangely," I continued. "They have both changed their ways and have a different awareness. I feel they needed lots of healing after they passed."

I could see clearly that the young man was touched from what I was sharing. The revelations from his friends had obviously softened his heart.

He approached me at the end of the evening to thank me. He told me that not only was he was shocked and amazed by my insights, but it made him think about his own choices. He said that his friends' advice would help guide his future decisions.

Spirit wants us to have loving, happy lives; lives filled with meaning and joy. Both of these friends recognised their own mistakes and wanted to make amends. Their guidance was intended to help improve their friend's outlook. Mediumship comes from a place of healing and love; always uplifting. Spirit's main focus is to prove life after death with the intention of helping. Those listening should remember that we are never alone. We are all subject to spiritual influences; loved ones who want to help us when the need arises.

Both of these friends' communications were intended to have a positive influence; to bring out the best qualities in those they loved. They had allowed their egos to wastefully direct them. However, when they passed, their souls had awoken. They realised the hurt their choices caused. The progression of their souls was evident by the fact that they wished to pass on this knowledge.

They wanted to communicate that we are here on this earth, simply to love.

CHAPTER TWO

Baby Story

I AM STANDING on another platform, facing a new crowd. Already, I sense the energy change around me.

I scan the faces and announce, "I have a little baby boy in Spirit. I know he never got out of hospital. He's looking for his mother in the room this evening. I can see him being treated on a life support machine. He was born into this world slightly premature. He didn't reach full term. There was a defect around his precious little heart. He was three days old when he passed to spirit."

I look around the packed room to see where this baby takes me. "There's a girl there." I point to a pretty young woman, thirties maybe, long blonde hair. "Can you relate to this?" I ask.

Her eyes well up. "Yes," she replies.

I continue with the link from her son in Spirit. "This is going to get very personal – are you okay if I share everything?" From the vibe her son's soul is giving me, I know that this woman has come through some extremely tough times.

"Would you like to join me on stage?" I ask.

People begin to applaud as she gets to her feet. I beckon her to me.

I continue the dialogue with the child: "Your son is making me aware that soon after he left our world, your relationship with his father collapsed. During the pregnancy you didn't trust him. Emotions were up and down. There was drama in that period, especially given his involvement with other women. He knows his dad wasn't fully committed to you in the way a woman would want."

The information keeps streaming into my psyche. "You loved his dad but the man wasn't able to meet your simple needs. The child knows you found it hard to deal with the lies. There was no trust."

"You have regrets. Whilst you were pregnant, you went along with your partner to parties; drinking and living life to the full. Is that the truth?"

"Yes, yes, it is," she sobs.

"After the baby died, you were riddled with

guilt. You blamed yourself for the excess. Your son keeps saying 'mummy you've nothing to feel guilty about.' You made choices; tried to keep up with his father's behaviour. You wanted to work things out, but deep down, you knew he wasn't good for you."

She's nodding agreement with everything I'm openly sharing, still weeping uncontrollably.

"It took superhuman strength to pull back from that relationship," I press on. "You had to get your life back. Sometimes you ask: *"Why did God take my son?"*

Dollops of tears drip down her face. The whimpering softens but persists.

"Your baby left us," I declare. "But the child's soul gave you the strength to escape the man's clutches. Your boy says that if you had stayed, you wouldn't be here today. You endured so much mental abuse before the pregnancy that you even contemplated suicide."

"You didn't plan to have him, but your baby knows you wanted him dearly. He is aware of that. He is your little angel in Spirit."

"Last night," I announce, "I was doing some art in my room. Your son came to me and told me you'd be here tonight. He wanted me to draw this for you." I reach to the back of a table on stage and begin to unwrap a painting. A long white feather is in the centre.

"All of this connects to the feather I placed on the canvas," I soothe, giving the frame to her.

Crying, she lifts her sleeve and shows everyone her arm. There are tattoos from wrist to elbow of feathers. All of these, for the memory of her son. Everyone in the room begins applauding, supporting this unfortunate woman.

"'Your son knew you'd be here tonight. He keeps mentioning the names Thomas and Tommy."

Bending over with emotion, she cries out, "That's his name and my daddy's name."

"Well, know that is his proof to you. Such a young soul, who spent just a few days here on earth. His only purpose in life was to save you; to enable you to walk away from abuse. That's why he's here, to share these thoughts. He wants you to be done with regret and shame. He is saying 'I love you just as you are mummy'."

Take his love and memory. Know he is with you always.

CHAPTER THREE

Introduction to Mediumship

MY NAME IS Angela Dunlop and I have worked as a Psychic Medium for the past eighteen years. It's an unusual career choice. It's not about tricky hocus-pocus, but real experiences every day. It's not frightening; in fact, it's the opposite. My work involves a loving interaction which allows me awareness and insight into the lives of strangers.

The entire purpose of having this gift is to provide evidence of life after death. I've seen how this ability can transform and empower.

Irish people have had this gift for centuries. The country's mythology is littered with tales of wise men and women who sat by camp fires, surrounded by tribe folk who gave forth visions of the future. It's strong in our veins, even though most of us have forgotten the knowledge our ancestors possessed.

These mystic descendants attained the same insights that I do when I work, enabling the

sharing of extraordinary experiences and perceptions. I believe that my insights come from
working with that same Spiritual power.

As a small child, I had a fascination with magic. I'll never forget the time I received my first
conjuring set. It was Christmas morning, and I
can still feel the excitement of unwrapping this
wonderful present. I devoured it, practising my
new found skills straight away. I even presented
magic shows for my family. Dressing up for the
occasion, I used my mum's housecoat as a
magician's cape. Waving my wand over a fan of
playing cards, I performed inexplicable feats for
my three younger sisters. Dazzled by my insights,
the look of surprise and amazement on their faces
thrilled me.

As a child however, I had no idea that mediums existed. Whilst I was happily showing off my
magic tricks, little did I know that there is a True
Universal Magic: a force that is transparent. It's
the power of love and healing which communicates telepathically through feelings and
thoughts.

For some, this can be seen clairvoyantly. A
miraculous power which brings souls together to
help us remember that human beings are not

alone, not even in death.

The miracle of mediumship is a form of heavenly magic which focuses on communication between the living and the departed. It comforts people in times of grief, dispelling the illusion that physical life is the end.

As a medium, I collaborate with Supernatural power. I share information from loved ones in Spirit with those who are living; knowledge which is evidence that their loved one is with them. I am privileged to be able to pass on personal details from the soul of the departed to the person for whom I am reading.

Individuals living in the physical world are looking for the truth and have burning questions. *Is my loved one safe? Are they content, happy? What do they do when they pass? Do they watch over me? Are they still around?*

I'm the intermediary for Spirit people. Whilst doing my best to concentrate on the flow of information streaming into my mind, there is an awareness of another soul's intimate memories and personality. All the while, I hold a conversation with the person or people in front of me, passing on the counsel their loved ones in Spirit wish to share.

A medium is like a telephone. I share telepathic communication between the loved ones in Spirit to the recipients in front of me. It's a humbling experience when I relay the details of someone's memories; their character, personality, family episodes, loves and fears.

Giving private readings on a daily basis has given me a special insight into the Spirit world. People assume that after a loved one dies, they have gone forever. It can be a wonderful surprise and relief when they receive contact beyond the grave. It is then that they discover the Spirit is keen to share memories and love.

Throughout this book I will be sharing real life stories, anecdotes and accounts from those I have done readings for. My hope is that you understand that the Spirit world exists and surrounds us at all times. I want you to know that Spirit loves us unconditionally. They see what we've been doing since they passed. They desire to help and comfort us in challenging areas of our lives.

This is a book to help restore your faith. I am going to share genuine tales from normal people who have proof of contact with their loved ones passed. Spirit loves each and every one of us. They care for our well-being and wish only the best for us.

They don't want us to worry or have anxiety. They especially don't want us to ruminate fearfully about their existence around us.

Spirit wants to prove to us they are safe and free from illness, disability or addictions. They want us to know that they are with us anytime we need. Their love for us can never be taken away.

It is eternal.

CHAPTER FOUR

The Sceptic

SCEPTICS ARE NOT unusual in my work. Over the years I've been heckled, judged and criticized for my practice. I remember one man running me out of his shop, red-faced and screaming because I asked to put up a poster advertising my event. I didn't entertain his anger; I simply walked away, albeit a little shaken.

I understand that mediumship challenges our beliefs and thoughts. Perhaps some people don't want to accept that we have a soul. They don't like the thought that discarnate souls exist around us. However, mediumship can lead us into great transformation; giving us meaning and purpose. It can help us to recognise our spiritual nature; to take responsibility for our lives and happiness.

At times, I come up against people's religious backgrounds. Not everyone is happy with their perception of 'raising the dead'. Some think that I'm 'taking away from a soul's peace'. And yet, it is so clear to me that Spirit wants us to know they are here. They have a strong desire to help us. They seek to encourage us to have balance and peace. They choose to reach out and remind us that we are deeply loved; that we aren't alone. When I commune with souls departed, I stay true to the experience and the feelings the 'Power' is giving me. To me, the 'Power' is God's essence; the loving energy working through me. This exchange of energy makes the contact happen, for the greater good.

I've learned to accept people's opinions or doubts. Suspicions and disbelief come with the job. Negative scepticism is something I have to deal with maturely and respectfully. I don't force my work on anyone; they will feel an attraction towards it. I believe Spirit will lead them to me or another medium. It's important to seek a medium who has a good reputation.

Most people I encounter are open minded. They hope that 'something' or 'someone' is helping them from the Spirit side. I work with integrity and love; both towards my sitter and towards Spirit. Honesty is so important; people need to feel able to trust the words I impart. My clients have a desire to be reunited with loved ones passed; to know they are still with them.

I simply tune into their loved one passed and share my experience. The Spirit world and those who love them will try their best to prove their existence. The true purpose for mediumship is to be a catalyst for the individual. After receiving a reading or being present in a demonstration, they have the choice to accept that the soul is a reality.

I've had clients who I've given detailed evidence of loved ones, but at the end of the day, it's their choice whether to believe. They have to come to their own conclusion. I can't force my opinion on anyone. I simply share my truth in the hope that it stimulates their curiosity and ultimately leads them to the truth.

A reading can prompt confidence that I am indeed in touch with 'something' loving, but even the most specific evidence-based reading can be rejected. People have their own choices whether to believe.

Throughout my career, I have learned to lean on my Spiritual senses; my visions, the auditory words I hear from Spirit. I have taught myself to tune into my internal awareness when a soul is blending with me.

At the end of the day, it's me having the experience. I try my best to explain my perceptions with the intention of helping. I seek to be open, empathic and compassionate towards the people I work for, on both sides of life. I do my best to creatively describe the Spirit's person identity, character and personality. This is what they are, Spirit people.

✧   ✧   ✧

IT WAS LATE winter and I was beginning my flow of readings after the Christmas holidays. My readings are always booked months ahead. My mum and the workers in the shop only take first names and contact numbers in case we need to reach them. I always prefer to read people that are strangers to me, it's much easier than some-one I know and I tend not to read for those closest.

I had just finished a one-to-one reading and was making a cup of tea in the kitchen before my next client arrived. I heard a man's voice in the shop. He introduced himself as 'Mr Patrick'.

'There's my client,' I thought, and I popped my head out to acquaint myself. I noticed how nervous he was which wasn't uncommon. Lots of people are afraid – usually because of religious backgrounds or fearful television horrors. I think he was surprised not to see an old lady in a puff of smoke!

"Mr Patrick?" I asked.

"No. Mr McGreevy," he answered.

"Oh, I thought I was reading for a Mr Patrick", I replied, looking surprised and wondering what was going on with the bookings.

"I am Mr Patrick," he admitted. "I'm on Facebook and I didn't want you checking up on me."

I laughed. The notion that he thought I had the time to check up on clients' social media amused me. "I can assure you," I grinned. "I don't need to be looking up people's Facebook pages."

"Come up to my room," I politely invited him. We walked up the two flights of stairs and suspiciously he followed. We both sat down on the black small leather seats facing one another. I began to tell him what to expect generally from the reading and that loved ones passed will do their best to make contact with him.

"What do you expect from today?" I engaged him, offering him the chance to open up a little to me. I find it easier to work with clients who are relaxed and not as uptight.

"I'd rather not say Angela, to be honest," he responded. "I'm not really sure why I'm here and I must admit, I don't believe in any of this."

I looked at him curiously, wondering what losses he had gone through to bring him to my door. "Well, let's give it a go and see how we get on. If you feel you haven't gained anything from the experience, you are free to walk away and keep your money."

"Perhaps I am curious because three people recommended this all on the same day. I thought that was odd and perhaps it was some kind of coincidence?" he openly admitted.

I'll let Mr McGreevy share his experience of what happened that day:

The session took place around late January /early February 2017; several weeks after my mother (Anne) and my aunt (Margaret) passed away.

I had always thought of card readers, palm readers and psychic mediums as charlatans. Snake charmers. Headcases. Nut-jobs.

Perhaps I was looking for something, or to reassure my internal know-it-all bloke that I am correct and this is all a load of crap!

After my dad passed away in December 2015, I found myself wondering if there was something he wanted or needed to say to me. This sense of post-loss wonder was very different when my mother passed away in December 2016.

I never felt I got a chance to speak to her at any great length (or depth) during the last year of her life. She was terminally ill.

I wanted so much to speak with her. Selfishly, I wanted to talk about me and her; mum and son; about our life together. I guess I pulled back on several occasions. I didn't want to cause her any emotional distress.

It was immediately after she passed that I wanted to talk to her. I recall asking, "Now this has happened, can I connect with you? Can you let me know you are in a good place?"

Every day without my mum, I asked her if she was okay. I asked her if she was with dad. I asked her if she was with her parents.

I was seeking a connection; needing some peace of mind and contentment. Searching for ways and means to make it happen, I looked for signs.

It was during my first day back at work that three different people recommended I visit a psychic medium. Was this a sign? A message?

Initially, I balked at the idea of sitting down with a psychic. One person who made the recommendation had recently lost a loved one and spoke of a 'wonderful experience'.

I thought about it for a number of days. Why would three people say the same thing to me on the same day? Was I projecting something? Did they understand what I was going through?

I began looking into the very thing I once mocked and belittled. I began to ponder the possibility of going one step further. What harm can it do? I'm not going to burst into flames, am I?

I found a quaint little shop in Belfast's Smith-field Market area called the *House of Healing*. It turned out that the shop belonged to one of the psychics recommended to me.

Opening the door, I was greeted with a cluster of scents. There were books about healing and mindfulness. Angel cards, crystals, aromatherapy products, candles, pendulums, and even angel figures surrounded me. None of this stuff was of any interest to me. I recoiled and left the shop.

After a coffee and a prolonged flick through a nearby vinyl record store, I returned with a second wind.

"This is all a bit of joke, isn't it?" I asked the woman behind a very small counter.

"No son, not a joke. I came many years ago for a reading and ended up working here because I love Angela and what she does for people."

Angela Dunlop is the *House of Healing* owner; a psychic medium. She wasn't in her shop when I called in; she had gone to pick her child up from school. *Seems normal enough,* I thought.

I plucked up the courage to make a booking – albeit with a false name. You can never be too careful in this social media age!

"I don't believe in this," I told the lady. "I don't know why I'm here and I don't know why I'm giving you my hard-earned money."

I had a few weeks to reconsider such was the demand on Angela's diary.

I returned.

So, there we were, in a large room with a small table and two small sofas, positioned beneath an old Casement style window. The room seemed a little soulless.

Or was it?

Angela had a big smile and perfect white teeth. She also had a broad strip-the-paint-off-the-walls Belfast accent. She explained what she did and asked what I hope to gain from the conversation.

Angela stared over my left shoulder. She told me there was a small woman who I was very close to, standing at my side.

"She's wagging her finger. She's telling me she's the one who says it as it is and you're the one who always stood by her."

Angela had no idea my aunt Margaret had suddenly passed just a few weeks before my mum.

"She's demanding the stage here. There are other people who want to say hello, but I will go back to this woman. I have no name for her just yet, but she's a strong and fiery wee woman, that's for sure."

My shoes were shuffling beneath the table and I was starting to shake in them.

During the session, I had no fear of challenging Angela. I also tried to make it as difficult as possible for her by maintaining a poker face (whatever that is, I don't play cards!)

She asked me about America.

"Come on, every Belfast family has someone in America."

She came up with the name 'Kitty' for my grandmother.

"Come on Angela, every Catholic home had a grandmother called Kitty or Kathleen."

She mentioned I had an aunt Mary, passed.

"Angela, every Catholic family has an aunt Mary."

I wasn't going to tell her that my granny was actually called Kitty/Kathleen and that I did indeed have an aunt Mary passed over.

She accurately described all of my grandparents.

And then…

Angela began running her hands from her ankles to her shoulders. Up and down, up and down.

"This is a real lady. This is a proper lady; well-presented, very well mannered, well-educated. Proud. I mean a proper lady. She's telling me she has a big family – I'm getting four and four; four girls and four boys. Eight children? Wow. She really worshipped you all."

Angela began running her right hand down the inside of her left arm. Then pushing her hair back from her forehead.

"That's my son."

ANGELA DUNLOP

Is this your mummy? Annie, Ann, it's Anne
with an 'e'. I feel like she has only passed within
recent weeks?"

I wanted to say yes. I couldn't. I simply
couldn't get the words out. I was frozen. Stunned.
Overwhelmed.

How does this woman do this? How does she
know this?

She described my dad too, perfectly.

"He's sitting beside you, laughing, nudging
you, and smoking. He's saying 'you can't stop me
smoking now, I'm enjoying a cigarette'."

There was so much more Angela told me
about my parents, immediate relatives and
ancestors; so much detail that she couldn't
possibly have known. How could she know such
finite detail?

She didn't know that my heart was breaking
because the very next day my uncle Jim, who I've
idolised all my life, was leaving Belfast. He was
returning to live in America with his family after
the sudden loss of his wife. His wife; my aunt
Maggie – the woman Angela first described.

"I don't think I recall so many people coming
forward for one person. You obviously have a
close family and you are very much loved.

Remember I mentioned America at the start of this conversation?" Angela shared.

"I do, yes, but America could mean anything. I go there every year."

"I have one last thing to say to you about America. This wee woman who has been here from the start, she's telling me she's called Maggie. She is saying to you, Jimmy is going to be okay, that you don't have to worry. Do you know what that means?"

And with this, I was an emotional wreck; exhausted, drained. I don't mind admitting that tears streamed from my eyes.

After ten minutes alone in the room, I composed myself and thanked Angela on my way out.

"I know you're a sceptic," she said. "But I hope you got something from this. I hope you find comfort. You have good people around you."

Red-eyed, I rushed to my car, after grabbing a coffee and a peanut-butter donut. I could have eaten fifty donuts. I felt like I had no weight inside.

Every day for weeks afterwards, I had so many different emotions, but there was definitely comfort. I was relieved to know that my loved ones were together in a good place; pain-free and happy.

Has this helped me dealing with grief? I think so. I think this medium fitted.

✧   ✧   ✧

THE MORE THAT Alex's loved ones relayed evidence of their memories with him, the more his disbelief began to melt away. Mediumship isn't just about the evidence however; it's the presence of love. Power and energy are transferred through me. Spirit does the work; I am just the channel. I simply surrender to their subtle insights.

Alex was overwhelmed with the accuracy. I hoped the reading brought Alex peace, knowing that his loved ones were safe, happy and together.

That's all I want for anyone.

✧   ✧   ✧

STEVE, A PRIMARY school caretaker, came to one of my demonstrations with his fiancé. Steve's father had left the family home when he and his sister were young. As a result, Steve had been looking for his dad for ten years.

For years, Steve's mum assumed dad must have died. However, there was no proof and Steve couldn't accept it. He never gave up hope looking for his father. He paid for private detectives who checked up on dad's whereabouts. His longing to connect with his dad kept him searching for years. They explored every avenue, but found no leads. Steve felt hopeless and disheartened at times; unsure if they'd ever track him down.

Where had he gone? Where was he living? What was he doing? Did he even want to be contacted?

Unfortunately, Steve finally uncovered his dad's death certificate. He had passed away in Dundee. It was a devasting blow to Steve, who had been hoping to bond with his father. Now he'd never get the chance.

Steve's fiancé booked tickets to come and see my work. Steve wasn't afraid to admit he was an out-and-out sceptic. A practical, down-to-earth man, he believed himself to be level-headed with no interest in mediumship or psychics.

Reluctantly agreeing to go along, he made sure to inform his wife-to-be: "Unless I see, hear or feel some proof, I won't believe it."

I noticed them arriving late and discreetly taking their seats at the back of the room. I was mid-flow with another contact, but immediately saw Steve's father from Spirit in my mind's eye.

Bringing my other contact to a close, I went directly to Steve.

"There's a man at the back of the room. I can feel your dad standing next to you."

I pointed at Steve. "You sir, with the moustache and goatee beard. Can you relate to your father passed?" I asked, already knowing the answer.

"I didn't know my dad," Steve responded stubbornly.

I reached for a sip of water, gathering my thoughts for a moment.

"That's strange, because your dad is standing next to you. If I give you a few pieces of information, would you know some details?"

"Yeah, I know a few bits and pieces," Steve reluctantly agreed.

"I feel he went to England to live and work; would you know this?"

"No, he lived in Scotland," Steve said flatly.

"Okay," I carried on, knowing that I'd come back to my observation again. "He's giving me the name *Bill,* can you relate to that?"

"Yes! His name is Bill!" Steve exclaimed, stunned.

"I know you said he lived in Scotland, but he's talking about travelling to England with his work. I feel his job took him around the UK. Would you know this, sir?"

"Yes, he worked in London," Steve confirmed, surprised.

"Yes, he's saying he lived in England for a while, with work."

"You might be wondering why your dad is with you today," I ventured. "He's here to say, *'Son I love you. I really love you'*."

"He's showing me that he had moved out and went on to have another family. He admits he was more present in their lives. It pains him to say, he gave them the attention you would've wanted. They considered him to be more of a dad than you would've done. He realises the resentment and hurt this caused you."

"He may not have known you in person, but he wants you to know he's with you now. He knows that you tried to find him and were hoping to restore a relationship."

"Yeah, I spent quite some time looking for

him," Steve replied softly.

"He's really sorry he wasn't there for you, but he wants you to know that he's with you now in Spirit."

Bill stepped back from my mind's eye and the link gradually faded.

Afterwards, Steve and his fiancé came over to chat to me. Steve told me that he had come in as a sceptic, but had to admit, everything I told him was true.

Steve was both shocked and elated to discover his father's presence and love. The whole experience was deeply emotional and uplifting.

"I'm really intrigued," Steve admitted. "It's heartening to know the journey isn't over."

The journey is never over for any soul. We continue evolving. Our soul's essence transforms from physical life to eternity.

"I feel settled and comforted now, knowing he is with me."

The reading transformed Steve from being lost and lonely to feeling comforted and cared for. That's the power of mediumship.

CHAPTER FIVE

Upbringing

IT WAS ONLY later in life that I discovered my aunt had the same gift for seeing and feeling spirit as me.

I was a happy baby with big brown eyes and naturally curly hair. Every day, my mum and I visited Granny Doyle's. There was an air of sadness and grief in granny's house. Mum's sister Christina died the year before I was born. She was only twenty-two, leaving behind her daughter Michelle, aged one and a half. Granny helped to raise Michelle.

Granny lived in a small three-bedroomed council house. With very little money, granny and grandad did their best to supply food and clothes for the family.

Granny had experienced a lot of tragedy unfortunately. Her own mother died when she was just a young child. Then, later on in life, after marrying my granddad, they lost their first son.

Little James died of pneumonia when he was only one and a half.

Christina, the most sensitive of the children, was also a medium. She shared a double bed with her two sisters, my mum Bernadette and sister Maureen. Christina was afraid of the dark, demanding that the hall light was always left on. She would wake up and scream during the night saying, "There's a man at the end of the bed!" When the lights were turned on, of course no-one was there. Adamant, she described him as tall, wearing a trench coat and carrying a small black case.

My grandfather, Richard Doyle, thought it was all a load of nonsense. He was a practical man who had worked hard all his life. He had been away at sea on the navy for many years. He told them all to "get to sleep!"

My granny thought differently. She wondered if Christina was seeing her father. None of the children had never met her dad, but he did wear a trench coat. He also used a black case to carry his paints – he worked as a sign-writer for local businesses.

Christina's experiences continued most nights; seeing spirit people in their bedroom. The lights were always left on at bedtime to settle mum and her sisters' nerves.

This wasn't the only experience of hearing and seeing spirit in granny's house. Mum, Christina and the young sisters would often hear whispers downstairs even though everyone was in bed. They even heard the sound of footsteps up and down the staircase.

Granny's sister Lily, who worked as a nun, could also see spirit people. She travelled around the country, helping orphanages and schools. Lily was able to see colours emanating from people, sensing their auras.

Granny's other sister Margaret was able to read tea leaves. Granny could read them too, but she only did it privately for close family and friends. Coming from a strong Catholic background, readings were frowned upon. Granny certainly didn't want an angry priest rocking up at her door!

Mum and Christina had a great fascination of the afterlife, but they wondered why these people kept appearing to Christina. Rather than appreciating the gift, it frightened them and they didn't like it. They turned to the church, hoping that if they prayed for people's souls, the 'ghosts' (as they called them), would leave Christina alone.

After Christina met her husband Michael, she moved out of granny's home and moved into a flat close to Granny Doyle's. Soon after, she gave birth to their daughter Michelle. Despite moving away from the house with the 'ghosts' in, Christina's spirit visions kept recurring.

About two months before my mum was due to get married, Christina announced to mum: "Michael's grandmother keeps appearing to me. She just keeps smiling at me. Do you think this is a warning about something?"

"No, she probably needs your prayers," Mum answered. They both assumed that when a 'ghost' was trying to make contact, they just wanted prayers.

Christina called into my granny's house one evening. Granny saw a white glow around Christina's head. She thought it was really strange and couldn't understand what it meant.

The following evening, Christina passed away to spirit. At only twenty-two years old, she died in her sleep. She had been out that night with Michael for a few drinks and took two sleeping tablets before going to bed. The coroner reported that she'd had an extreme reaction to the tablets that sent her into a coma, and then death.

Mum was devastated; in complete shock, as was the whole family. What about the white glow? And Michael's grandmother appearing in spirit to Christina? Was that a warning? Did they miss something? Was there something she was trying to say?

Trying to pick up the pieces of Christina's loss, mum focused on me and brought me to visit granny every day.

When I was around nine months old, I was happily playing with my toys, when mum turned to granny and said, "I'm just going to change Angela here." She lifted me in her arms and walked up the stairs to granny's bedroom. As Mum sat me down on the bed, her name 'Bernadette', was heard as clear as though someone was speaking aloud. It was my aunt Christina's voice from Spirit. My mum darted her gaze across the room and back to me to see if I heard it too. My brown eyes widened and I glanced across the room to see who it was. The room was empty.

Shocked, mummy picked me up and ran downstairs, screaming to granny. "There's someone in your room trying to talk to me!"

This wasn't the first (and it certainly wasn't

ᴛne last) time my mum and I would hear spirit voices. However, it wasn't until I was in my early twenties that my journey into mediumship would begin.

Mum didn't talk about Christina while I was growing up. There was a black and white photograph of her sitting on our television. I used to look at her photograph and think about her. It was only later in life that I discovered my wonderful aunt had the same gift as me.

Early Childhood

WE LIVED IN an area called Cherry but mum didn't like the small house. Heavily pregnant with my second sister Lisa, we needed a larger home to accommodate our growing family. Praying to Our Lady, mum asked for help with housing.

Mum had her first spiritual experience when she was only five years old. She was sitting on top of the family piano, gazing out the window at the fields and trees. It was then that she noticed a young lady dressed as a nun.

"Who's that lady?" mum asked granny inquisitively.

"What lady?" granny answered, following her child's line of vision.

Mum pointed towards the young nun who stood smiling at them.

"There's no lady there", granny scoffed, brushing off the question.

The words "Saint Theresa" popped into mum's mind.

There was a painting of Saint Theresa (commonly known as 'The Little Flower'), in Granny's bedroom, but mum recalls the lady in the painting looked nothing like the woman she had seen.

In the small house in Cherry, a free magazine popped through the letterbox one day. It was called 'St. Theresa's Mission'. Out of interest, mum flicked through the pages. She recoiled with shock. Mum came across a photograph of the saint in her younger days. It was the exact image of the young nun that came to her in early childhood.

Taking this as a sign, mum prayed for a new home. My mother, a lady with great faith in prayer, had her prayers answered. Miraculously, a stranger called to our home and asked if we would like to swap houses. The new house in Twinbrook would become my home for the first fourteen years of my life.

In our new home in Twinbrook, Christina tried to make contact with mum several times. She stroked her hair and called out her name, but mum would scream when it happened. She recoiled from any contact through fear and lack of understanding.

By the time I was eight, I had three more siblings: Lisa, Theresa and Bernadette. At only twenty-four years old, Mum had a lot on her hands. My dad, Tommy, was a painter and decorator by trade, but he would take any job to bring the money in. Work was scarce and there wasn't much money. However, Dad had a head for business and was always cooking up ideas to try to earn cash.

One of his ideas was selling fish around the neighbourhood. He'd been a fishmonger when he was younger and knew where to buy the fish wholesale. He bought a small white van and every Friday, we would have crates of fish stored in our kitchen. He'd weigh it, put it in bags and get it ready for sale. Our house stunk! We didn't care though, my sisters and I would help him selling the fish around the houses.

We would call door-to-door asking neighbours if they wanted to place an order. Then dad would deliver their collection. I loved working with him. We would package the fish up in white plastic bags. When they gave me the money, I usually got a tip of twenty pence. By the end of the fish run, I might have gathered up a couple of pounds! Added to that, dad always gave us fifty pence payment for helping out.

One Friday evening, he called at his friend's home with his regular delivery. The friend wasn't in so, thinking he was doing a good turn, he put the fish through the letterbox. Two weeks later, that same friend caught up with him and told him he was going to kill him. He said that he had been away on holiday for a couple of weeks. When he returned home, it stunk of rotten fish and maggots!

Over the months, Dad also introduced apples, oranges and pears to his fish run. My sisters and I loved this. We played shop with all the fruit in the front bedroom. We loved to play imaginary games. Although we didn't have much money, we always got lots of toys at Christmas and shared them with one another. We loved our bikes, dolls and board games. They were happy times. I had to share a double bed with Lisa, but I didn't mind. I liked the comfort of having someone in the bed beside me. I was afraid of the dark and used to feel like there were people in the room.

I remember waking in the middle of night and feeling someone sit down on the bed beside me. My heart was pounding. I lay frozen. I didn't move or say a word. Whatever it was, it went away and eventually I fell asleep.

A shy, quiet and sensitive child, I gravitated towards a caretaking role. When my mum needed help with my younger sisters, I tried my best to lend a hand. We would play out in the streets with the other kids, but I always worried I didn't fit in. I felt different and lacked confidence. When money was tight at home, dad would get stressed, drinking and shouting. It was difficult to listen to his angry outbursts.

Deciding to join the church choir, I hoped that it would help my anxiety. Having always escaped my emotions through music, I learned to play the tin whistle and fell in love with it. I discovered an ability to be able to listen to music and then play back what I heard. A local community group needed new members so I joined in. I was even asked to play the opening theme tune for a popular television show called 'Blue Peter'. I had a wonderful day meeting the presenters and guests.

Playing my little flute helped to ease my anxieties. Living through 'The Troubles' in Belfast, I had a constant fear that my parents might get shot. When they went out for a few drinks on a Saturday night, I was terrified the bar would be bombed. It was such a relief when I heard the key turn in the lock and knew they were home safe.

Threats of paramilitary violence, recurring riots and civic conflict led to a programme called "Project Children". Set up by Americans, it was an organisation who wanted to help young children. They wanted to show the kids a different way of life; a life that could be inclusive of both sides of the community – Catholic and Protestant. The selected few would have an opportunity to stay with an American family for six weeks.

I'd never been abroad before. The furthest I had travelled to was a seaside town called Carnlough, where we had stayed in my aunt Maureen's caravan. I already had the travel bug at that age because I loved getting away from my neighbourhood and experiencing a different environment. My teacher, Mr Hogg, announced that one girl and one boy would be picked to go to America. He just needed to know who was interested and if they had parental permission.

I ran home as fast as my tiny legs could carry me.

"Mummy, mummy can I go to America?" I burst into the kitchen where she was sitting chatting to my aunt.

Mummy took a drag on her cigarette and carried on chatting, obviously not realising the magnitude of my excitement.

"Mummy, Mr Hogg said you just need to fill this permission letter!" I interrupted her chat again. "And then I'll be able to go to America! Please! Pretty please!"

Laughing at my excitement, she took the piece of paper. "I'll ask your daddy when he gets home," she appeased me, still unsure of what I was talking about.

Hoping with all my young heart that he'd say yes, I awaited his return home from work with anticipation. Waving the piece of paper at him the minute he got through the door, imagine my delight when he scribbled his signature at the bottom! He said yes!

When I brought the slip of paper back into school, I discovered that, of course, several others in the class wanted to go too. They also had their signed permission slips. The teacher decided to pop all the slips into a hat and pick one lucky winner.

I just knew I'd get picked.

I watched him put all the names into the hat, waiting with trepidation and excitement.

"And the winner is…"

My teacher looked around the class at all the eager faces.

"Angela!"

I was picked! Absolutely exhilarated, I couldn't wait to experience flying on an aeroplane and travelling to another country. It was one of the most memorable holidays I've ever had.

CHAPTER SIX

Joe's Story

AS A MEDIUM living in Northern Ireland, I come into contact with many individuals who have lost loved ones to 'The Troubles'; a thirty-year-long conflict that engulfed the country. Belfast's city centre was out of bounds and to venture outside your own territory, was to risk getting a bullet in the head.

It was even too dangerous to travel in a taxi. Paramilitaries would pose as cab drivers. To give your address meant that you were exposing your religion. When he asked "Where to?", your address could literally be the difference between life and death.

As a result, the youths mingled within their own district, congregating in neighbourhood bars. To drink in the town centre risked a death sentence, so business boomed for local pubs.

Local residents witnessed paramilitaries handling rifles or petrol bombs on a daily basis.

Bursts of gunfire were heard regularly. Curfews were in place. Paramilitary defenders would fortify themselves in people's gardens, hiding behind the walls. Gunmen loitered in neighbourhood alleyways, ready to attack. Living in the middle of a civil war, it was a scary time. People feared for their lives.

We were used to the British army parading the streets in our neighbourhood. The sound of the green army trucks was distinctive. Sometimes there were six large police jeeps parked on our street.

As a young child, my friends and I would gather around the British soldiers who were patrolling our street. They let us scrutinise their ammunition. A policeman allowed us to glance through the lens of his loaded gun, seeing far into the distance.

Houses were often raided for bomb making equipment. Police would patrol the streets with guns and radios looking for signs of terrorist activity. Violence often erupted when the police were around. Groups of children and adults threw bricks, bottles and petrol bombs.

My sisters and I weren't allowed out when trouble erupted. My mum wasn't strict but naturally, she didn't want any of us getting caught up in the middle of the conflict.

It became natural to see violence regularly. Almost three thousand, six hundred people died during the thirty years of 'The Troubles'. The television was flooded with ongoing antagonism between Catholic and Protestant politicians. Headlines showed innocent people being murdered for no other reason than their religious background. I have vivid memories of Dad shouting at the TV during the six-o'clock news; his anger directed at politicians. As a young child, reports of terrorist activity frightened me.

People were encouraged to phone a confidential hotline to disclose terrorist activity. TV adverts tried to warn young men against joining the paramilitaries. I can still remember one such ad showing a boy growing up just like his dad. Scenes of a father and son walking down a flight of stairs; a gunman opening fire on the dad, the son watching in horror as his father was murdered right in front of his very eyes.

When my mum and dad went out for a drink on a Saturday night, I was petrified I wouldn't see them again. I remembering crying to my mum, afraid they might be killed in a bomb.

For thousands of people living through the 'Troubles', thankfully, peace eventually came. The 'Good Friday Agreement' was signed on 10th April 1998, ending most of the violence. It was a major development in the political history of Northern Ireland.

I remember the day well; the sound of car horns blasting, the roads lined with hundreds of cars, all showing their support. Paramilitary groups in Northern Ireland were finally surrendering to a new way of living. Talking and resolving their differences; leaders had decided to come together for the sake of peace and protection for future generations. There was a widespread overwhelming feeling of relief.

Growing up through the 'Troubles' has given me the ability to relate to people from different communities and traditions. I work with people from all backgrounds, creeds and colours. In Spirit, there is no religion; no cultural divides, societal leanings or judgement. Spirit's intention is to remind everyone that they are loved, valued and remembered. As a medium, my role is to be non-judgemental; to remain open to each and every person I come into contact with.

Spirit wants to create unity between people,

communities and countries; *not* separation. Mediumship is inclusive of all family back-grounds.

Over the years I have met many people who have lost loved ones to 'The Troubles'. Here is one such story.

Joe

IT WAS 1973 and newly pregnant Mary went to visit her brother in hospital. Accompanied by her husband Joe, they decided to walk instead of getting a taxi. Little did Joe know; this would be his final walk home.

As they headed up Stockman's Lane, they knew they were taking a risk. Everyone knew that if you were walking in that direction, it meant you were Catholic.

Unbeknown to them, they were being watched. A white car sped up behind them. One man was driving and another man jumped out. He shouted at Joe to get his attention. When Joe turned around, the man lifted his gun, pointed it towards Joe and shot him in the head.

Mary screamed loudly, running towards her husband and cradling him in her arms as he was passing away. The gunman simply laughed at her reaction, pointed the gun once more at Joe and took another shot at him. He died in Mary's arms. Their unborn baby would never see his father's face or get to know who he was.

Forty-five years on, I'm looking into the eyes of this unborn child. He introduces himself as Joe. He has brought his wife Annemarie and daughter Jolene for a private family sitting.

I enjoy family readings. It's an opportunity for the whole household to receive spirit that are relevant to all of them.

"I wasn't even meant to here, love," Joe broadly declares.

"Oh," I beam, knowing there's no such thing as a coincidence. It is always meant to be.

"Yeah, my other daughter was meant to come down today. She couldn't make it so I took her place," Joe shrugs.

"Well, perhaps it's meant to be," I smile. "Let's go upstairs to my room and see what's happens."

As we sit down, I explain how I work. "Today is an opportunity for you and your loved ones to connect with Spirit. Please be aware that it's an experience that flows through me. You may have more than one communicator from Spirit. Before I begin, I always close my eyes and pray to God and your loved ones that you receive what you need from this experience."

Immediately, I sense Joe's scepticism. I can tell that his suspicious mind is closed towards me. I'm used to people's apprehension however, so I don't allow it to put me off. I invite them to remain open during the reading.

I close my eyes and stay silent for a few moments. In my mind, I can clairvoyantly see a gun. I can also see and feel a man. I know he's Joe's father.

"Joe, I feel your father here. He is young and passed away many years ago," I begin. "I keep sensing the era of the troubles with him."

Joe shifts in his chair, looking uneasy. "Yeah, my Da passed, and it was during the troubles," Joe agrees hesitantly.

"He's showing me that two men were in the car. One shot at him."

Joe's eyes fill with emotion, as he nods in agreement.

The information keeps pouring through me. "'I feel his name is Joe too."

"Yes, I was named after my father," he confirms.

"I am now being taken clairvoyantly in my mind to West Belfast, particularly, the Whiterock area," I tell him.

"That's where our family live," Joe states, somewhat surprised.

"Your daddy is showing me, in particular, the area of Ballymurphy," I state.

"Yes, that's where I grew up!" Joe answers, stunned.

"Your daddy keeps taking me back to the Ballymurphy name. He shortens it – does the surname Murphy mean anything to you?"

"That's our surname!" Joe reveals, with excitement and enthusiasm.

"So, your father is Joe Murphy from Ballymurphy?"

"YES!" Joe declares excitedly. All his defences are down now. Since I'd never met them, his scepticism is truly dissipating. He knows I am somehow connecting to his father.

"This is fantastic," I say to all of them. "How amazing are your dad's memories?"

They grin in agreement.

"There's a granny here with your dad. She was a tough granny but loved you like a son. Patrick is here too," I tell them.

"Oh my god, Patrick was like a brother to me!" Joe breaks down with emotion. "My granny raised me and Patrick. He died young too," Joe reveals.

"Your daddy is showing me that you drive a taxi for living," I look at him.

"Yes, that's what I work as," Joe confirms.

"He is saying that you had a previous car where the head gasket blew in the engine. Your daddy was trying to give you warning signs to sell the car."

Joe's earlier tears turn to surprised laughter. "All of that is true. I did drive another taxi and the gasket blew up two years ago."

"Just know that it's your dad's way of letting you know he has been with you," I reassure him. "Your daddy is saying to keep a check on your back, right hand tyre."

Joe nods in agreement. It was a little while later after the reading was over, that Joe told me he discovered a puncture in the same tyre!

Laughing with Joe, I then looked at Annemarie and Jolene, shooting them an apologetic smile. "I'm really sorry this reading is all for your husband."

Annemarie smiles simply, "I'm glad, he needed this."

Joe chuckles. "I told them before we went in that I'd be the star of the show."

"Let's keep going," I press on with enthusiasm. "You must all love going to Portugal. They're talking about you going. You love returning to the same place time and time again?"

"Yes, we've been going to Portugal for years. We're going back again this year," Annemarie agrees.

"Jolene, your granddad in spirit is saying that you're looking for a job in childcare."

"Yes, I've applied for work in a local school as a childcare assistant," she confirms, surprised.

Bringing my attention back to Joe, I tell him, "There's a baby boy here in Spirit with your dad."

His eyes full of emotion, Joe opens up. "That makes sense. It must be my brother. My mum had two previous losses before I was born. One stillborn, and one who died a few days old."

"I feel your dad wants you to have faith. He wants you to heal from everything you've been through. Your reading was evidential, to let you know he is around you. He loves you and is with you always."

CHAPTER SEVEN

Gabrielle

"YOU'RE PREGNANT," THE doctor announced, after testing my urine sample. Even though he confirmed what I already knew, I didn't feel ready for this massive change.

"How old are you?" he enquired, his expression not hiding his disappointment.

"Twenty," I told him. Although uncomfortable with his disapproval, I knew I'd do my best.

Mel and I had been seeing each other for three years. To be honest we weren't getting on. Our romantic bubble had burst and we were constantly arguing and bickering. I was trying to make it work but knew intuitively it wasn't going to last. How was I going to cope with a baby on my own?

We were so young when we met. We hit it off straight away, falling in love quickly. With his swarthy complexion and Italian looks, I was drawn to him immediately. I was in one of my favourite clubs when I spotted him. Although jumping to the beat of the music, he glanced over towards me and held my gaze for a few seconds. A fuzzy electric feeling sizzled through me. Eyeing up his black hair, moustache, white t-shirt and jeans, I was extremely attracted to him.

He glanced over a few times, catching my eye. He must have felt something too as I could see him making his way through the crowd towards me. Nervously, I looked away, trying not to pay too much attention to his oncoming advance.

"Would you like a drink?"

I noticed his brown eyes. "Yeah, sure," I smiled, trying to appear confident.

He leaned in towards my ear so I could hear him over the loud music, "What's your name?"

"I'm Angela," I smiled.

"You look gorgeous," he said.

Yes, so do you, I thought, but I kept that to myself.

Over a thousand sweaty people roared to the next tune, dancing with glow sticks in the air. The smell of Vicks lingered in the atmosphere from the raver's white gloves. It was the 90's and I loved the buzz of getting ready each weekend; the excitement of going to raves. I would travel with my sisters to hear famous DJs in different towns. It was all about the music, boys, clothes and parties; going out with friends, enjoying life freely.

One of my friends was an amateur DJ and had turntables in his bedroom. We would hang out and play records. I loved mixing decks and trying to beat-match tunes in sync. I wasn't too success-ful but my desire to DJ was getting stronger.

"I'd love to be a DJ," I told my sister. "I think it'd be amazing to play music for thousands of people." She didn't take much notice, but I was serious. I started collecting a few records myself but with little money, it was wishful thinking.

"I'm having a party in my house afterwards; would you like to join us?" Mel pointed to the crowd of friends he was with.

"Yeah, I'd love that."

It had all started so simply, and now here I was, walking home, trying to absorb this preg-nancy news on my own. What will mum and dad say? They won't be happy. Mum would be so disappointed.

I didn't want them to know straight away. I was still living at home and mum had enough worries. Granny Doyle was unwell. She was in and out of hospital and the family members were taking turns to care for her.

There was an enormous amount of tension in our home. Dad and mum weren't getting on, and neither were me and Mel. I wasn't working at the time and was living off government benefits.

I plucked up the courage to tell Mel the pregnancy news. I thought he'd be devastated, but to my relief, he was over the moon! *Perhaps things will change now,* I thought hopefully.

Granny Doyle passed away the following month. Naturally, the family was devasted; mum in particular, as they were extremely close. Granny had struggled for a few years with different health complaints. I battled with feelings of guilt, beating myself up that I didn't make enough time to see granny towards the end of her life. As funeral arrangements were being planned, I kept my pregnancy a secret. My sister Lisa had also found out she was pregnant a few months earlier and mum was already focused on her. I didn't want to add to the stress she was already under.

I worried about how we were all going to fit into a three-bedroom terraced house. Six adults and two new babies; it was going to be tight.

When my nephew Alan was born, I fell in love

with him as did everyone in the house. It was good preparation for me; helping me get ready to look after my own baby.

I couldn't hide my growing bump any longer. I had to pluck up the courage to reveal my pregnancy.

"Mummy, I have something to tell you," I said anxiously, biting my lip.

I just blurted it out. "I'm pregnant."

I expected a slap in the face; an angry outburst, but no, there was no such reaction. Mum looked shocked; she was quiet and distant. I didn't know what was worse.

"Okay, it will all be okay," she said eventually, taking the news in slowly.

I was more nervous of my dad's reaction, but thankfully mum quietly reassured me; "'I'll tell your daddy."

She broached the subject with him when they were at the swimming pool. They had taken baby Alan along for a splash around. Perhaps she knew it was best to disclose the news when they were in a public place; he could hardly cause a fuss if they were surrounded by strangers, Thankfully, he took it well. The relief washed over me – now everyone knew.

As my pregnancy progressed, I had recurring dreams. I was a DJ, standing in front of crowds and audiences, playing to my heart's content. I still day-dreamed about owning some equipment so that I could start practicing. However, in reality, my growing bump meant that I needed to push those ambitions to one side and take driving lessons instead.

It was summer, one of my favourite seasons, and I loved learning to drive. I enjoyed focusing on the road in front of me. It helped to take my mind off all the worry and stress.

It was the night before my driving test. Foreboding the outcome that I might fail; I went to bed praying. I tried to be hopeful, but it was easy to slip into worry. I fretted about most things, particularly about my relationship with Mel. We were still arguing. I wondered if the pregnancy would settle us, but he grew distant and our relationship was on and off.

That night I had a dream; my driving instructor rang to say that his car had broken down. He needed to borrow a friend's car for the test. In my dream, the new car was a red Ford Fiesta. It was the same make and model as the car I had been practising in. The only difference being, was that the one I had been driving was blue.

In my dream, I saw myself passing the test.

When I woke the next morning, recollections of my dream came flooding back. *It must be a wish fulfilment dream,* I thought.

Getting out of bed, my thoughts were focused on the day ahead and the upcoming test. My driving instructor was due to pick me up for another lesson before we made our way to the test centre.

Ring, ring, ring, the phone echoed around the house.

"Angela," Mum shouted. "Phone call for you."

I ran downstairs, curious as to who was ringing so early.

"Hello?"

"Hi Angela, just wanted to let you know I'm running a little late. We've had to switch cars. My car has broken down and won't start. Don't worry though – I'll be there to bring you down for your test," my driving instructor reassured me.

My mind raced back to my dream, shocked by the similarities.

"You'll still have time to practice," he continued.

"Umm, that's alright, but will I be able to drive the new car okay?"

"Yes, of course, it's similar to what you've been practising in. I'll see you soon!" he chirped back cheerily, hanging up.

Slightly dazed, the nerves really kicked in. I started to freak out, what if that dream came true?

"Mummy, that was my driving instructor – I'm doing my test in another car. I had a dream last night that this would happen."

"Maybe it's a sign," my mum smiled simply.

I darted back and forth from the bedroom to the living-room, nervously waiting for him to arrive.

A red car pulled up outside and I spotted my driving instructor sitting at the wheel. As I approached the car, I noticed that it was indeed a red Ford Fiesta; just like I'd seen in my dream. The same make and model.

This is weird, I thought.

When we arrived at the test centre, I was horrified to discover that the examiner's nickname was Zorro – on account of the number of fails he dished out.

I drove the test route as best as I could. When it was over, I parked up and he turned to face me.

"Congratulations, you've passed!"

I jumped out of the car to tell my instructor the good news. Smiling and happy, I eagerly blurted out about the dream I had. He probably didn't believe me, but I didn't care – I was thrilled!

"I passed! I passed!" I shouted, as I ran up my street, smiling from ear to ear. Mum and dad were working in the garden and heard my cries of delight.

When I settled myself, I began to think back on the dream. I knew it had been a premonition; a glimpse of the future. How did I know what was going to happen? Intrigued, I thought about all my family members who were mediumistic and had spiritual gifts. *But me? No.*

I'm not psychic, I couldn't be! I thought, putting that notion to the back of my mind. Anyway, I wanted to be a DJ, not a medium or psychic!

The months progressed and winter was setting in. My time to give birth was fast approaching. Excited but nervous at the same time, my bump was growing, as was the love developing for my unborn child.

A week before the birth, I started having contractions on and off. Then I felt them coming stronger. Another sharp pain. *This is it*, I thought. *I'm going to have a baby.*

"Mummy, I think we should go to the hospital now."

Mum had watched me all night as we timed the contractions.

Oh my god, I thought, freaking out. The fear had kicked in – worry about the labour, anxiety about how much pain I'd be in. Would the baby be healthy? Would Mel still be interested in me? Would he love his baby? Would I be a good mother? Would I be able to cope?

Snatching my hospital bag from the bottom of bed, I waddled towards the front door. Dad was watching television.

"Daddy, we're heading to the hospital now. What do you think I'll have?" I asked him jokingly, trying to put on a brave face.

"A girl," he replied, grumpily.

"Well, I'll let you know soon enough," I said, walking out the door.

Instinctively, I felt I was carrying a girl. I just knew.

I had prepared as best I could, purchasing what I could afford over the prior months. I had opened a credit union account so I could save money for my new arrival. Family members helped out too.

On 28th November 1998, on a cold, bright Saturday morning, Gabrielle Christina was born. I gave her my aunt Christina's name in her memory. With her swarthy complexion and black curly hair, she was a perfectly healthy baby. I was delighted. I had never experienced love like it. My life felt completely fulfilled. Although I experienced the bond with her immediately, I fell deeper in love with my new bundle of joy every day. She was perfect in every way.

CHAPTER EIGHT

DJ Miss Innocence

THE RECURRING DREAMS of being a DJ were happening almost every night. As a new mum, I tried to suppress my ambitions. After all, Gabrielle was only a few months old. *That's not what young mums do,* I told myself.

"Set of turntables with mixer and a hundred dance records for sale," an advertisement jumped out at me. Excitement raced through my veins. Even though I knew my mum would kill me as I still lived at home, I had that inner 'ding' moment; an intuitive voice that told me to go for it.

I had very little cash and was only receiving benefits, however I still managed to save a few pounds. I was hoping to purchase a car at some point and was stashing money away for that.

When I read the reduced price for the equipment, my mind was made up. *I'm going to buy them. I'm not going to tell anyone; I'm just going to go get them.*

I knew my mum would be against the idea. She didn't want noisy dance music pumping through the house, especially with a young baby around. I could see her point, but I was adamant. I decided it was best not to tell her as she would only try to deter me.

I booked a taxi to take me to the seller's house. When I arrived at the guy's door, he was surprised to see a young girl standing there. I was only twenty-one and there weren't too many female DJs around. Determined, I didn't let this put me off.

"Can I have a look at the turntables you have for sale?"

"Come on in, love," he replied in his thick Belfast accent.

He had everything set up for me to practice. Admittedly I hadn't a clue what I was doing. I had a few sessions on friends' turntables, but that was just for fun. This was the real deal.

Trusting my dreams and instincts, I decided to go ahead and buy them. *Fake it until you make it*, I told myself.

"I'll take them," I announced confidently.

Arriving home with all the equipment, mum's face said it all. She wasn't one bit impressed. But I didn't care, this was what I really wanted to try. Thrilled to bits, I had a clear vision of standing in front of crowds, sharing my love of music.

With a young baby and a growing passion, I balanced being a mum and practicing DJ skills. There wasn't enough space in my bedroom so I had to squeeze all the equipment under my bed. Everything was crammed into a small double bedroom; Gabrielle's cot and toys, along with my bed and drawers. I did manage to keep some semblance of tidy order though. When I wanted to practice, I spread the decks across my bed and when I was finished, slotted them underneath again.

After only six months of practicing, I was asked to do a gig.

Strolling through HMV, I perused their large selection of records. Sifting a little of my fortnightly money, I carefully selected a couple of tunes. I loved the feeing of the records and felt so excited to mix them together. I kept visualising myself playing to crowds in large clubs.

One of the shop workers noticed me. It wasn't every day a girl pushing a pram was scrolling through the latest tunes.

"How long have you playing?" he asked. "I

see you in here all the time."

"I just started about six months ago," I told him.

"Do you want to do a gig in the Limelight?"

Stunned by his invitation, I beamed inside. The Limelight was an extremely popular local nightclub.

"Okay, I'll give it a go," I replied nervously.

We arranged the date and set a time. I was going to be the warm-up act.

It can't be that hard, I thought. *I'll just practice my set.*

"Do you have a DJ name?" he asked. "For the posters?"

"A DJ name? No, not yet," I replied, as confidently as I could. "I'll let you know."

As I pushed the pram home, I kept thinking what name I'd give myself.

DJ Angela? DJ Angel? No.

DJ Miss Innocence. Because of his paranoia, Mel was constantly accusing me of flirting with other men. I was always having to protest my innocence.

Trembling with nerves, I turned up for my debut a few weeks later. Mel, my sisters and a few friends came to support me.

My earphones were low-priced and not a great quality for clubs, so I borrowed a pair of professional earphones from another DJ. I was hoping to upgrade my own equipment when I had the money.

Shaking with adrenaline, I plugged my earphones into the mixer. I set my first record on the turntable and switched on the button. *Nothing. No sound.*

What is going on? I anxiously fiddled around with the buttons. *I can't hear any music!*

I adjusted the earphones again and accidently snapped the cord. *Oh god, what have I done? I've wrecked their equipment!*

Like a deer caught in the headlights, I urged one of the guys to come and have a look.

"I don't know what I've done! I think I've broken it!"

The first record was coming to an end and I was meant to be mixing two records together. Panicking, I couldn't hear a thing. I hit play on the next record as the man tried to solve the problem. He couldn't fix it either! He called their sound engineer – even he couldn't fix it!

I had jammed part of the headphones and broke it off completely. I stood at the side of the stage, mortified. They had to shut the music off completely while they changed the equipment. It was a disaster. Not the start I was hoping for!

As time moved on at home, I was getting a little frustrated living at mums. Although I appreciated her support, I really craved my own space and independence. Thankfully, Mel and I were offered a council flat nearby. It was a two-bedroom ground floor flat which had been newly refurbished. We managed to get what we needed for our first home.

I was also thinking about going back to work. I had a little experience in clerical work, having worked in an office temporarily. Although I had enjoyed it, my real dream was to be a DJ. Luckily, I was getting the odd gig here and there.

Scanning the newspapers for jobs, one jumped out at me. An organisation which helped disabled adults in the community. It was perfect. Our role at the Disability Network was to help clients to socialise and be inclusive; creating opportunities to get outdoors and join in activities. I had to create newsletters, carry out clerical duties and help on social outings. I loved it. It was such a joy to be involved in a caring role.

Although I was really happy in my role helping people, my relationship with Mel was taking its toll. The stress of living together became very apparent and we were on and off all the time. I loved being a mum and Gabrielle was all I cared for. I just wanted to create a calm and happy life for the two of us.

"Listen in this Saturday night for a chance to win a set of turntables and a mixer."

My ears perked up when I heard the announcement on the local radio. The equipment I had was basic. I knew that if I won the new turntables, it would help me to play in more nightclubs. My stomach flipped with excitement; I just knew I was going to win.

Poised and ready, phone at my side, I listened attentively that Saturday evening. The presenter kept building up the excitement as the show went on.

"When we play Alice Deejay, call our studio to win a brand-new set of turntables."

Oh, just hurry up! I thought, excitedly. The minute the first few bars of the song played, I snatched up the phone and immediately punched in the number. The line was busy! I tried again, and again, and again. Each time, the dull tone told me that someone else was already on the line.

Finally, on my next attempt, it rang! The presenter answered chirpily, "Hello, Q radio?"

Ahh! I got through!

He asked a simple DJ question which I knew straight away. Answering correctly, he happily congratulated me – I had won! I was ecstatic – my ambitions of being a club DJ were now starting to come true.

Meanwhile at home, the turbulence of living with Mel was becoming too much. He was fed up too. We weren't happy together and our lives were miserable. I had stayed far longer that I should have, but I was doing it for Gabrielle's sake. I thought she needed to have her dad around. However, I realised that my own mental health was beginning to suffer and so, we agreed to end things. Although painful, I knew it was for the best in the long-run.

The next couple of years as a single mum were difficult, but every moment with Gabrielle was joyful and fun. Bless her, she fretted for me anytime I had to leave her. I really wanted to improve our lives. Even though I enjoyed my part time job, I didn't earn a lot of money. I tried to balance being a mum with trying to find opportunities to play gigs. I had a few DJ gigs under my belt, but I was still an amateur DJ. I had managed to build up a small record collection and I kept my equipment in the boiler cupboard.

Needing a bit of fun, one of my friends invited me to an *Ann Summers* party. It was a girly night of fun and games, with a chance to purchase some lingerie and toys. I got chatting to one of the girls and the conversation veered towards Spirits. She spoke to me about her father passing. Telling me about an experience she had at the Belfast Spiritualist Church, my tummy fluttered with excitement and intrigue. I couldn't get it out of my head. Contacting her, I asked if she would bring me along. My sister and a few friends went along with me to the Sunday service.

I didn't know what to expect. Everyone looked normal. There were prayers and hymns like most churches but there was one difference. A lady got up on a rostrum to prove evidence of loved ones who had passed.

Lisa and I giggled through most of it. The laughter was probably due to nervousness. I was secretly hoping my granny would come through, but she didn't – not on that occasion. Neither of us got a message that night, but I was so intrigued. How could she stand up there and do that? Was she really communicating with loved ones who had passed? Did it not frighten her? How did she know so much information about people?

As we left, I was fascinated and something kept drawing my attention back to that church; the atmosphere, the medium, the spirits. I wanted to go back.

CHAPTER NINE

First Connection

THE BELFAST SPIRITUALIST Church really intrigued me and I wanted to go back. Was it only out of interest – or was there another reason?

A lovely lady greeted my sister Lisa and me. We were given hymn books and directed towards the seats. There were rows of chairs, all facing a small stage. Taking in my surroundings, I noticed that most of the chairs were already filled. There was a lovely feeling of peace in the room.

Everyone was chatting quietly among themselves until a side door opened and a small older lady appeared. She approached the lectern smiling and introduced herself.

"Good evening, you're all very welcome here. My name is Marie Pead and I am the President of the Belfast Spiritualist Church." She spoke softly with a welcoming tone. A set of principles were read out, followed by a hymn and then prayer.

There were more hymns, followed by an inspirational talk. And then it was time for this ordinary looking woman to tune into some sort of mystical power.

There wasn't a puff of smoke or crystal ball in sight.

As she stood on the platform, she gazed off for a few moments into the distance. Nodding her head, it looked like she was talking to someone in an otherworldly realm.

Whatever she was experiencing, she seemed ready to impart her insight with us.

Finally, she began sharing her communication with departed souls to us.

Listening, I noticed the evidence she was proving. There was a mixture of names, personal memories and knowledge of how the person died. She was able to describe what the living person has done since their passing; proving that the loved one passed still sees us and still watches over us.

For some individuals she went direct to them with a message. For others, she described the Spirits coming through and asked the congregation if they knew them. She appeared to be in touch with something heavenly.

The messages she passed on were loving and

uplifting; words of encouragement. She was able to provide evidence of people's memories and details of their lives; validation that their loved ones in Spirit were communicating.

This lady is talking to the dead! I thought, amazed. *Incredible! How does she do that? Is this truly factual?*

The audience seemed to believe her. Some cried when they received connections, comforted by her words and details.

Fascinated and intrigued, I remained open minded. I hadn't received a message and to be honest, I think I would have been too afraid. I worried I'd have frozen to the spot if she came over to me.

As the evening came to a close, my ears perked up when there was an announcement about an awareness class for beginners. It was held every Monday evening in the church.

Something lit up inside me. *I need to go.*

"I'd love to go to those classes!" I nudged my sister Lisa. "Do you want to come with me?"

"No, definitely not for me," she responded defiantly.

The next day, even though I couldn't get the thought out of my head, my inner desires were being swamped by fear. *I've no one to go with. I might look foolish. Why do I want to go anyway? Maybe it's silly.*

I didn't know why I was going. I had no interest in being a medium and I certainly didn't consider myself to have psychic ability. But something drew me there. I decided to give it a try.

I had no excuses about transport or childcare. I had just bought my first car, a cheap Ford Fiesta I had saved long and hard for, and my sister Bernadette agreed to babysit Gabrielle.

Driving over, I reached the doors of the church and took a huge breath before stepping inside.

I shouldn't have been worried. Marie gave me a warm welcome. "Come and sit down," she smiled, with a twinkle in her eye.

A circle of chairs was laid out in the middle, with about twenty students seated.

Embarrassed to turn up alone, I sat down, trying not to give anyone eye contact.

What I am doing here? I thought, mortified. I couldn't wait to leave, even though I just arrived.

Relaxing music was playing in the background and Marie began to lead everyone in a short meditation. I had never meditated before and had no idea what to do.

"Just relax, allow yourself to be in a place of stillness," I heard her say.

I'm not relaxed at all, I thought, waiting patiently for permission to open my eyes again.

After the meditation, she gave each of us a sheet of white A4 paper. Markers and pencils were laid out on the floor before us.

"Choose what colours you're attracted to and draw some symbols," Marie advised.

Unsure what this exercise had to do with being a psychic, I followed her instructions, scribbling a few triangles and squares.

Marie then asked us to pair up. "I want you to swap drawings with your partner and see what you feel about the other person."

I was expected to give a reading of the other person by looking at the symbols they drew!

Looking around, I observed the people in the group, wondering who I could pair up with. There was a mixture of ages, but I was the youngest; only twenty-four.

One girl approached me. "You new here?" she asked. *She must be psychic!* I thought.

"Yes, I am, I replied nervously. "Do you want

to work together?"

I wasn't sure what Marie wanted us to do but I gave it a go.

"Feel the impression of the symbols," Marie was saying. "What are they saying to you about the other person? Trust your feelings."

My partner looked at my symbols and began, "I can see you've come through a bad break-up. I feel he wasn't faithful to you over the years. He really hurt you and you now find it hard to trust people. Does that make sense?" she asked.

Shocked at how she was getting all that from a few triangles and squares, I nodded my agreement.

"He gave you a tough time. Has he got another child now?" she asked.

"Wow, you are really good at this," I confirmed. "Yes, he has another daughter." How could she know so much about me from a simple drawing?

"I feel you're going to be really good at all of this," she said, waving her hands around. "With mediumship."

Ah, she hasn't got this part right, I thought. "Maybe," I said hesitantly, although I didn't really believe it.

When the evening ended and we said good-bye, I walked away, reflecting that it hadn't been too much of an ordeal. Nothing scary happened – I wasn't tied up and put on a stake! If anything, I felt a lot calmer. It was lovely that someone understood what I had gone through. I resolved to return the following week.

During the following weeks, I began to look forward to the Monday night classes. I was excited to try out the exercises Marie gave us and I was beginning to relax into the meditations. I was also starting to develop new friendships.

Even though I was excited, I was still full of nerves. When asked us to introduce ourselves, I would squeak a reply, my face reddening and my heart pounding. If picked to do an exercise in front of the class, I was so embarrassed, I felt like crying. *How do mediums stand on a platform in front of an audience, holding a microphone?* It was beyond me.

Occasionally, there were guest speakers – mediums visiting from other towns. After only a few weeks attending the awareness classes, a medium from England attended. She started with a meditation, leading us into a place of deep relaxation.

To my amazement, during that meditation, I met my grandmother, my aunt Christina and my grandfather! I also saw a man dressed as a Native American.

My aunt Christina told me that she had been helping me for a long time. They were all offering me support and encouragement on my path.

When I came back into the room again and back to my full consciousness, I was brimming with emotion.

"I'd like you all to pair up with someone. Tonight, we are going to try mediumship," the teacher announced.

I looked around and spotted a young girl who was a similar age to me.

"Will we work together?" I asked. She nodded, smiling warmly.

Lifting our chairs, we found a private space away from everyone. Facing one another, we made some small talk as we settled.

"Choose who is going to work first," the teacher instructed. "When you've done this, close your eyes. Invite the Spirit world to come close to you. Be aware of any subtle feelings or visions; thoughts you may hear or have. Share everything you receive, just allow it to flow. Feel the power of the Spirit. Learn to make the link with Spirit."

I had never tried this before, but I trusted the teacher's guidance.

"Focus on what you see in between your eyebrows," she directed. "Your mind's eye; what you feel; share anything you are experiencing."

I closed my eyes and followed her instructions. Surprisingly, in my mind, I could see an image of a man. I decided to trust the impression.

"I can see a man," I announced to my partner. "He isn't very old, about fifty. He has a receding hair line. He is giving me a father feeling, does that mean anything?" I opened my eyes to see if she understood.

"Yes, my daddy is passed," the girl replied.

Shocked by her confirmation, I was also aware I could feel loads of energy around me. Thoughts were streaming quickly into my mind. I started sharing everything I was experiencing.

"My heart is sore; he is giving me pains across my chest. I feel like I am having a heart attack. He's showing himself in the kitchen making food. Your dad liked to cook, he was the chef of the family, not your mum."

"Yes, my dad loved to cook and he died of a heart attack," she confirmed.

"He feels like a very funny, warm, loving man. He loved you very much. He's showing me a gold bracelet he used to wear."

"Yes, my dad and I were very close," she confirmed again. "And he did have a gold bracelet."

"He's talking about you starting a new job in business. He's also aware that your car is giving you some trouble at the moment."

Smiling, the girl confirmed both statements.

"Your telephone line has interference. I feel that your dad is laughing. He's saying it's him."

She confirmed this too, informing me that they had engineers visiting recently to inspect the line.

"I'm getting a feeling of loads of love towards you. Your dad really wants you to know how much he loves you."

Suddenly, the contact started to fade. I became more aware of the room and my surroundings. The energy around me wasn't as strong. I became more conscious of the other students. I also noticed the emotion on this young girl's face.

"Are you ok?" I asked.

"Yes," she said, emotionally. "That was all true what you said. Thank you for that. My dad was in his fifties and he died of a heart attack. Everyone loved him very much."

I couldn't believe it! It was the greatest feeling I had ever experienced. There wasn't anything frightening about it. In fact, I felt an indescribable sense of joy. The ability to pass on a message; my first time communicating with Spirit. I was on a complete high!

Suddenly, I knew what our teacher meant by feeling the power of the spirit. I was hooked!

Although I continued working in Disability Network, I started to read up on my new found interest in spirituality. Fortunately, I worked very close to the local library. I borrowed books about psychics, mediums, meditation, palmistry and tea leaf readings. Anything that would enhance my abilities and help me to fine tune what I was being taught in class.

I would have butterflies in my stomach every Monday, such was my excitement. The classes became the high point of my week.

Marie, my teacher, was noticing my progress too. She even asked me to join her Tuesday night circle.

A circle is a dedicated group of people, usually around eight to ten individuals, learning to fully understand their gifts. It was an honour to be invited. As the youngest member, I began to learn the discipline. I was instructed to always be on time, to never miss a session (for any reason other than sickness) and to give everything a try. We were committed to unfolding our gifts for spirit. I agreed and began my training as a medium.

As my circle work began, Christmas was fast approaching. Gabrielle was only four years old and she couldn't wait for Santa to arrive. Lisa and I drove to the local toy store, loading up the car with her presents. Bratz dolls and accessories, games, a pram and a toy kitchen. Gabrielle loved watching the children's movie *Monsters Inc.* so I bought her the one-eyed green monster *Mike Wazowski.*

Arriving home, I hid all her presents in the shed, locking them away. Now that all her presents were bought, I could settle. Deciding to watch a Christmas movie with her, I felt it would get us into the festive spirit.

"Gabrielle!" I called up to her bedroom. "Come down and we'll watch a wee movie together." She ran downstairs and into the living room. Something distracted her and she pointed over towards the window.

"Mummy, the car is gone!"

"What do you mean?" I asked, confused.

"The car is gone!" she repeated.

"You wee tease, has it really gone?" I asked, jumping up from the sofa and rushing over to the window. She was right, our car was gone. Someone had stolen it.

Panicking, my mind raced. I had saved for a couple of years for that car! Who took it? Where is it?

I knew it was gone, but strangely, I had a gut feeling I would find it.

I rang my neighbour Sean, relaying the dreadful news. "Did you see anything, Sean?"

"No love, sorry. Do you want me to help you look for it?"

"Yes please! Let's look around the estate! Give me two minutes to get ready!" I quickly put on Gabrielle's shoes and coat, then sorted myself out. Sean was waiting patiently in his car for us.

"I don't know why, but I think we should try Cherry," I told him, referring to another area of the estate. As we made the short five-minute journey, I kept my eyes peeled, scanning everywhere for my car.

I saw a group of young lads hanging about and I asked Sean to pull over.

"Excuse me lads, have any of you seen a navy ford fiesta?" It was a common car, but I was so desperate, I thought it was worth asking.

"Yeah, I saw one parked up there," one of the lads informed me, pointing up the street.

Thanking him, we pulled away quickly.

"Go Sean, go!" I exclaimed.

As we screeched up the street, there it was, in all its beauty. My car. Sitting patiently.

"Oh my God! There's my car!" I shrieked. Not a single mark on it! The relief was palpable.

Looking over my shoulder, I noticed there was no-one around to witness me. Cautiously, I opened the car door, jumped in the front seat, and switched the engine on. By jiminy, I decided to steal it back!

Driving back to my apartment with Gabrielle in my now re-possessed car, I got indoors and rang the police immediately. They arrived a few hours later and took a statement. When they returned, they had uncovered the mystery.

The guy I bought the car from, had two keys and only gave me one. He brought the spare key to a party. One of the young lads decided it would fun to steal my car. Thankfully, he was arrested.

I knew I was being guided that night; right to the exact spot.

Little did that guy know I was developing my psychic powers!

CHAPTER TEN

Mediumship Training

"NOT EVERYONE WILL be a platform worker," our teacher Marie began. "Some of you may go on to be healers; some might prefer to do private sittings; and some of you may be called to work in churches."

I loved attending circle; training in mediumship became the high point of my week. There were ten of us; all willing to be of service and dedicate our time to Spirit.

Marie was preparing us, in whatever way our gifts unfolded. Although she never pointed out our specific abilities, her encouragement was always felt. It was up to us to individually discover our paths.

I was excited to learn how mediumship worked. How could I use my abilities to help others? How could I discover what talent I have?

Although still very shy, something happened when I worked with Spirit. I felt empowered by the Spirit world. Their love and energy flowed through me. Always doing my best to understand what Spirit was sharing, I learned to surrender to the information I was receiving.

"Mediumship takes time to evolve," Marie reminded us. "It's not be rushed. Mediumship takes many years to blossom. You are learning how Spirit are communicating with you. Trust your impressions. Surrender and let go of doubt."

"It's about moving into the experience," Marie encouraged. "Staying present with the information you receive. God works through you. God's power is the conduit for mediumship. You are the channel, Spirit blends with you."

"Remember, mediumship is an awareness of Soul-to-Soul communication. Their soul blending with your soul. That's what gives you the knowledge to share memories of a departed soul's life."

"You've got to train your mind to be quiet. Still your thoughts from daily activity, concentrating only on what Spirit wants to express. Spirit will work subtly through you. Learn to be receptive. Allow yourself to get to know your own Spirit and guides."

"You will be aware of your aura changing as

their soul touches your auric field. You may feel energy around you. Temperature changes. Colours, lights or symbols. The feeling or awareness of loved ones or guides. This is all normal," Marie reassured us.

In the circle, we sat together in meditation; disciplining our minds to focus on our perceptions. My sensitivity was increasing as I began to have more internal experiences. I could feel energy and power around me. I could hear a loving voice inside encouraging me. I could see colours, symbols and spirit people.

Sitting in atunement every week was an important part of my development. I was learning to Spiritualise myself. My awareness opened to the knowledge that I am much more than just my physical body. I was getting to know my soul in the silence. I was aware of a Power greater than me which I began calling God or Spirit. This power felt like it was healing me during my quiet time.

As I relaxed into a place of stillness, I could feel my physical, mental and emotional energy being restored to balance. Using my breath, I learned to let go of my daily thoughts and worries. I began to feel the benefit of daily meditation.

"I want you all to keep an open mind," Marie instructed us. "This evening we will invite Spirit to blend with you. As always, surrender to any experience you may have." Marie began to play relaxing meditative music.

Closing my eyes, I began breathing deeply; in and out. As I relaxed my body, I put out the thought: "Come and blend with me, Spirit". I could feel myself letting go. In my mind, I could see beautiful shades of purple and pink. I breathed in the colours feeling floaty and tranquil. I kept breathing; expanding my energy in and out, moving with the colours.

As my awareness settled, the energy around me began to shift; it deepened. I kept breathing rhythmically. I began having visions of riding bareback on a white wild horse, on top of a red dusty mountain. The gallop of the hoofs gave me such a feeling of freedom; being outdoors in the wild. As I looked around, I could envision Native American Indians on horseback riding alongside me. They were happy to see me.

The Indians prompted me to join them. We rode together to their campsite. I could see white tepees. I sat in a tepee circle with indigenous elders, taking part in a sacred ceremony. The holy elders shared their peace pipe with me. As I passed it on, one of the Indians welcomed me. Tanned skinned, he had long black hair and was wearing a large white head-dress. This was my first introduction to 'White Feather'; an initiation to my Spirit guide.

Sitting at home for an hour each day, I began to regularly attune with Spirit and my guides. I created time and space for their presence to be known to me. I was never afraid; the experience always felt safe and loving. I became aware of other guides too.

'Chi' (which means energy), presented himself to me in a different meditation. I could hear a room full of men lovingly chanting. Wearing distinctive saffron robes, they were in a holy temple. Bowed on the ground, they were giving reverence to Source. I observed their ritual; feeling an infinity with them, admiring their red and yellow ceremonial dresses. I felt one of the monks blending with me. 'Chi' is an old man; a Buddhist monk. His presence always emanates patience and love.

I learned that most Spirit guides have had a physical incarnation. They understand human life; our strengths and weaknesses; the difficulties we may encounter. Their souls have a God-conscious background. Spirit guides are typically Egyptians, monks, Buddhists, church figures or Native American Indians.

Guides are committed to serving humanity; to awaken people to their spiritual potential. Spirit wants peace in our lives and minds. I came to understand that my Spirit guides were positive influences. My interactions have always been loving, gentle and supportive with them.

I was enjoying meditating. Not only did it calm my mind, but I was having some wonderful insights when I communicated with my Spirit team.

My sensitivity began to enhance. I was changing as a person. I didn't expect mediumship to become so joyful, but it was. Previously, I felt I had stumbled into mediumship; now I realised my soul called me to it. It was ingrained in my life like a vocation; an inner calling to explore. I was committed and wondered where my journey was taking me.

Emotional and physical changes were happening to me. I was going off certain foods and decided to give up alcohol. In my meditations, the guidance I was receiving to change myself was profound. Listening, I took action. It felt like I was shedding a layer of skin. There was an inner desire to reach as many people as possible. It was only early days in my development, yet I had great determination and enthusiasm to learn.

I became quieter and more withdrawn. My intentions, attitudes and outlook on life began to change. I was starting to engage in a real relationship with myself, feeling more gratitude, love and joy.

It was truly a time of healing. Becoming more self-aware of my thoughts and actions, I began to release the emotional pain experienced as a child. Letting go of old attitudes that no longer served me, I freed myself from self-judgement and from judging others. Positive changes were being put in place. It was a time of regeneration.

It was also a confusing period. I felt lonely at times. One of the crippling self-beliefs I carried with me, was that I was worthless. Needing to lean on those around me, I cried a lot.

These growth stages are apparently a very natural process to unfolding mediumship. Building myself stronger mentally and beginning a real relationship with myself, were all necessary attributes.

In time, I started to gain confidence. My self-esteem began to flourish and I felt more alive than I had done in years.

Our teacher Marie asked us to keep a mediumship journal; a record of what we were experiencing. I had kept a diary throughout my teenage years and I enjoyed writing, so I began jotting all my experiences down.

The anxiety about my career niggled at me. I didn't enjoy clerical work; my passion was still being a DJ. And yet, I felt an attraction towards personal readings. Even though the calling was there, it was dampened by my fears.

What if I'm not good enough? What if mess up the information I relay? What if I look stupid?

Sitting in meditation, I decided to seek Spirit's guidance. Cross-legged on my sofa, I prepared myself for their support.

Breathing deeply and relaxing, I became aware of *Chi's* loving influence. Peacefully, I began communicating with him telepathically.

What is my purpose? Is there anything I need to do at this moment with my mediumship? Will you help me in my life? Will you show me the way forward?

Showing me images in my mind, *Chi* answered my questions with encouragement. I could see a Spiritual Centre on the Falls Road area of Belfast. He was indicating that this would be mine. I would work from this centre, carrying out readings, teaching and demonstrating.

You will help thousands of people from all walks of life.

His prophecy into my future was expansive, and yet my doubts held me back.

A Spiritual centre? Readings? Teaching people? Demonstrations? I'm still a beginner. I'm not even sure if I want to be a medium! How is all of this going to happen? I must be away with the fairies!

Chi told me write it all down, which I did when I came out of the meditation.

As much as I loved mediumship and the classes, I still wanted to be a DJ. I had started a few gigs in a nightclub called 'Union Street' in Belfast. I felt so confused about my future and I wasn't sure if I was getting mixed signals from Spirit.

A shop? Teach? Demonstrate?

I was thinking of doing a few readings but my guide's vision didn't fit in with *my* plan!

Not fully believing my power as a medium, I decided to go and have a personal reading myself. I was going to allow a professional medium to read *me*.

There was a brilliant medium, Brian, who I had watched at the Belfast Spiritualist Church. He had a great reputation for helping students, so I decided to book an appointment with him. I would listen to what my loved ones and guides wanted to tell me, through Brian.

Arriving at his office in Belfast, I climbed the steep set of stairs. I was welcomed by his assistant, who asked my name.

"I'm Angela. I'm here to see Brian," I said nervously, still slightly out-of-puff from climbing the stairs.

"He won't be long," she smiled. "He's just finishing another reading."

Sitting down and taking in my surroundings, I tried to relax. Pictures of goddesses and buddhas adorned the purple-painted walls and a smell of incense wafted in the air.

I had never experienced a one-to-one reading with a professional before. Sure, I'd had one-to-ones with the other students, but they were novices like me.

I wonder if he'll be able to read my mind?

Brian's door opened and an older lady walked out. She was clutching a hankie to her face, still emotional from whatever she had heard.

Oh my god! What if I cry? What if he's reading my mind? I better try to keep my thoughts positive!

Brian must have sensed my nerves. With his kind, soft tone, he invited me into his room. There was a sense of peace. I sat down on the leather sofa facing his chair. There was a small brown desk in between. Again, the walls were painted purple.

What is he going to say? I hope he doesn't tell me anything bad!

Spread across the brown desk, was a set of tarot cards. On one end of the desk; a cassette recorder. Popping a cassette tape into the machine, he asked, "Have you ever had a reading before?"

"No, I haven't," I replied, watching his every move.

He pushed two buttons together to record the session.

"I have your granny here," he started straightaway. "She's giving me the name Theresa."

Immediately, my tears started to flow. "Yes! That's her name! It's also my sister's name."

"She's proud of you," he smiled. "She's talking about you taking the path of mediumship – you *will* work as a medium. She can see you have a strong ability. It won't always be easy, but Spirit will keep you moving forward. Spirit has your back."

"She's showing me that you will work in a holistic centre. Someone will invite you to work there. You will do readings and teach there."

"I can see you leaving your current job and starting your career in mediumship," he stated.

Shocked, I was in awe that he was communicating with my deceased granny! Not only that, but she was confirming everything my guide had envisioned for me!

"Your Spirit guides are working hard behind the scenes to set everything up for you. You aren't to worry; your path has been laid out."

Brian's visions sounded wonderful, but I was anxious I'd have to give up the DJ work.

"Will I still be a DJ?" I asked.

Recognising my apprehension, he smiled reassuringly, "I feel you will carry on with some DJ work, but your calling is mediumship. You are a medium Angela."

"There will come a time when you won't be able to take on anymore bookings because you will be too busy. I can also see America and you writing a book."

Writing a book? Too many bookings? America?

This man has lost the plot, he must be talking about someone else.

Despite doubting Brian's visions, he then went on to accurately describe my granny.

"She's a feisty woman. I feel she didn't always get along with her husband, but she did love her children dearly. I feel there were five girls in the family. She rarely left the house and was incredibly protective. She's giving me the name Eileen and Patrick. She's telling me there's a nurse in the family."

"Yes, Eileen is one of the five daughters," I confirmed. "She's the nurse. Patrick is her son. She didn't always get along with grandad. He moved to England after their daughter died."

"She loves you very much," Brian told me. "You are getting a lot of help from Spirit, your guides and loved ones. In particular, your granny will keep you right with your path in mediumship."

Overwhelmed with emotion, I left his office.

That was amazing! How could he know so much?

Thoughts whirled around my mind as I walked away. His visions confirmed the messages I received in meditation!

Maybe Spirit are real! Maybe they are trying to help me. Maybe I need to learn to trust them more. Perhaps I am meant to be a medium after all!

CHAPTER ELEVEN

New Beginnings

PROPPING UP MY umbrella, I dashed outside. I was running late for work; nothing unusual about that. Even though work was only a ten-minute walk away, I still struggled to be on time. To be honest, I didn't have much interest in the office job any longer; I was ready for a change.

As I walked, my thoughts naturally reverted to my on-going concerns; worries about work, my future, my career. Snippets of Brian's reading were replaying in my mind.

You will work in a holistic centre doing readings. You will teach and help thousands of people.

It sounded like a pipe-dream. Fear and doubt plagued me once again.

How can I leave a steady job without an income? How can I get clients to come and see me? How can I set up a business? I've never managed a business before! I don't feel good enough.

The rain poured down heavily as I quickened my pace, glancing at my watch. By the time I arrived at work, it was ten past nine.

"You'll have to try to be on time, Angela," my manager Claire announced firmly.

"I know," I blushed. My unpunctual behaviour was obviously grating on her nerves.

Sitting at my desk, I appraised my duties for the day. It was always the same old thing – typing, filing, faxing and answering the phone. Deep inside, I knew that being a clerical officer wasn't my real passion, but I had no idea how I could make the transition to mediumship.

The centre bustled with activity; clients were playing games, making craft and drawing pictures. As I watched them having fun, my awareness suddenly shifted. A man from Spirit was standing right next to me.

What's going on?

At that same moment, the cleaner, Bernie, arrived to start work. I knew it was divine timing; the Spirit man had come for Bernie. I tried to act normal.

"Good morning Bernie," I greeted her.

"Morning, Angela," she brimmed. Bernie was always positive and cheerful.

"Bernie, this is going to sound a little strange, but there's a man here with me in Spirit. He's called Charlie. He's pointing to a box of chocolates and asking if you enjoyed them?"

Stunned at first, and then laughter erupting from her lips, Bernie answered, "Yes, Charlie was my husband's grandfather! When we were children, he used to bring a box of chocolates to our house every Friday night. The kids loved him!"

"I didn't know it at the time that I would go on to marry his grandson," Bernie continued. "We just knew him as *old Charlie*. It wasn't until I started dating my husband that I found out they were related."

"Wow! Small world," I smiled. "Obviously you were meant to meet."

"Yes, I know," Bernie agreed. "That's strange that he's coming through."

"That's all I felt from him," I told her. "He obviously just wants to let you know he remembers you and the chocolates. We don't always receive the connections we're expecting, especially this early in the morning," I laughed.

Amazed yet grateful with this titbit of information, Bernie thanked me and carried on with her daily cleaning duties. It was later on that day, after I had finished doing some paperwork, that I sensed another grandfather. This time, the message was for my colleague Cathy. I knew that Cathy was open-minded. I had mentioned to a few of my work colleagues about my mediumship training. Fascinated, they quizzed me on the subject.

Does it frighten you? How do you receive the information? Is it draining?

I reassured them that it always felt loving; their soul empowers both the sitter and myself. It's not draining or frightening at all!

"Cathy, I know I shouldn't be doing this in work," I said, sidling up next to her at the coffee table and keeping an eye out for my boss. "But I have your grandfather here."

"Oh really?" she replied, intrigued.

"Yes, are you okay if I pass on his message?"

"Yes, definitely," she agreed. "What's he saying?"

"Your grandfather is showing me that you keep a small grey teddy bear on your bed. He's telling me that he gave it to you when you were younger. The message from him is on the foot of the teddy – you can check it out."

"Yes, I do have a teddy he gave me years ago!" Cathy confirmed, surprised. "I'll have a look when I go home!"

The next day, she rushed excitedly to see me.

"Angela, I looked at the foot of the bear! It said: *Love Always!*" she expressed gratefully. "I know it was my grandad telling me he still loves me. We were very close."

Given the two connections at work and the fact I had received guidance from Spirit, I finally decided to take the plunge and began offering personal readings.

Spirit will always have your back, Brain's words echoed in my ears.

Spirit certainly had more faith than me.

Bernie and Cathy, the two colleagues from work, organised some people for me to do readings with. They arranged for them to come to my home for practice. It would be good for my training and experience.

The readings went well. I spent an hour with each person. I didn't charge them at first. It allowed me the freedom to experience the Spirit world without feeling pressurised by money. I started taking more bookings, practising from home.

Life felt like it was moving in the right direction. I was working as a DJ in Union Street bar on a Saturday night. I enjoyed it immensely; mixing house music and creating beats for party revellers.

One night, when I had finished my DJ set and was getting ready to leave, the head bouncer John stopped me. "Can I have a word?" he asked.

Following him outside, I wondered if I had done something wrong. Trailing behind this 6ft man to a less crowded area felt rather intimidating.

"I've heard you do readings for people," he said, shifting on his feet.

"Yes, that's right," I replied, somewhat intrigued.

"I'm going to open a therapy centre offering alternative therapies. I wondered if you'd be interested in renting a room?"

Ooh, so this is what he wanted.

Brian's words rang in my ears. *You will work in a therapy centre doing readings.*

Excited yet nervous, I was unsure if I could even afford the rent. Would I really be able to help people? Would I have enough clients to cover the rent and bills? Could I truly believe in myself? And yet, I had to admit that my practice readings were going very well, which was at least giving me a bit of faith.

I took him up on his offer.

I began offering one-to-one private sittings; putting out adverts and ordering business cards. The room was small, but sufficient for my work and I decorated it nicely.

Business was slow at first, but life was incredibly busy. Like a circus performer spinning a number of plates, I was juggling a number of roles: being a single mum, going to an office job every day, attending circle, DJ'ing at the weekend and starting a career as a spiritual medium.

It wasn't easy and I felt stressed a lot of the time, but I kept going. I felt that spiritual work was the right path for me and I was dedicated to it. I wanted to let go of the office job, but I knew it would take time. I needed the steady income until I built up my clients. My time and finances were stretched to the limit.

Over the next few months, I slowly built up my clientele. I did a lot of private one-to-one readings and enjoyed meeting people from all backgrounds and walks of life.

Finally, I was able to let go of the day job. I had built up enough clients to make the break, but it was terrifying. The office job had been my safety net; a financial anchor. Now, I was jumping into the unknown. I had to cling on to whatever courage I could muster and trust that it would all work out.

Everything was going well until I got an announcement one day from John the bouncer. He informed me that the owners wanted their building back and I'd have to give up my lovely decorated room. Disheartened and confused, my thoughts spiralled into fear.

What now? Where do I go from here? I've invested so much time and energy into this room, trying to build my business. Why did Spirit set all of this up, only for me to have to walk away?

By this stage, I had a steady stream of clients and I decided I'd have to use my home as a work base. It was difficult making the transition from work into home, with clients coming in and out of my house. Thankfully Gabrielle's dad helped with childminding; that relieved some of the pressure. The good thing about working from home was that it would alleviate some of the financial pressures. At times it felt like I was only living to pay bills, but at least now I didn't have to pay for an office space.

Taking up cycling as a stress buster, I actually

found I had more energy when I returned home from a bike ride. Lifting the bicycle up the steps towards my flat, I opened the front door and rushed inside to use the bathroom. Sitting on the toilet with the door open, I could hear sounds emanating from Gabrielle's adjacent bedroom.

"Hey! You over there!" I heard one of her toys say loudly.

Surprised, I glanced into her bedroom and heard another voice from the same toy. "I got my eye on you!"

Walking into Gabrielle's bedroom, I noticed the *Mike Wazowski toy* on top of her toy box; the one I had bought her for Christmas. I lifted the toy and shook it. Nothing. No voice. I pulled the arm down and it said, "*I got my eye on you!*"

Puzzled, I wondered how this one-eyed monster had been able to operate on its own, only several minutes earlier.

Just then, I felt the energy shift around me; the same feeling I get when someone in Spirit is close. It was my aunt Christina in Spirit. The incident with the toy was her joking with me. Along with her joviality, I could also feel a real sense of reassurance from her; that all the challenges at work would be worthwhile.

Deciding that I needed a bit of fun and relaxation, I took Gabrielle to the cinema. We loved going to the movies and usually went every week, catching up on the latest children's aminations. It was wonderful to enjoy quality time with my daughter.

Arriving home from our trip, refreshed and relaxed, I opened the front door and reached for the light switch. Stopping in our tracks, we heard voices.

Spirit whispers

Frozen to the spot, I looked at Gabrielle. "Did you hear that?"

Her look of fright told me that she had. She grabbed my hand. "Mummy, what was that?"

As we stood in the dark, more voices whizzed around the living room and into the hallway. I listened intently trying to understand what I was hearing.

Spirit whispers

It lasted only a few seconds, but we both heard them. Flicking on the light, I walked up the hallway, checking for intruders.

"Did you hear that?" I asked Gabrielle.

"Yes mummy."

"I couldn't make out what they were saying, could you?"

"I heard 'Be at peace'," Gabrielle revealed.

I wasn't scared; simply curious to find out what Spirit were trying to communicate.

"Be at peace," I repeated. "What does that even mean? Be at peace with what?"

By now, word was getting out about my readings and client bookings were flooding in. My modest flat just about suited our needs, but I was desperate to have a separate work space.

When the next appointment arrived at my door, I greeted the man and invited him in. He was broad-shouldered and robust with a stocky build. He came across a little hard and seemed suspicious.

"Come in," I showed him towards the kitchen table, where I worked from. We sat facing one another. My ginger cat, Tom, greeted him too, brushing alongside his leg.

"I hate cats," he shrieked, jumping nervously.

Laughing, I lifted Tom out of the kitchen. Sitting back down, I began explaining how I worked and tried to calm him.

I started *tuning in,* becoming aware of his father and mother in Spirit. As I started to relay pieces of information about his parents, he held a tough exterior; his face showing no emotion whatsoever. Even as I carried on, giving him more evidence that his parents were with him in Spirit, he still kept a stiff face.

This is a tough reading, I thought. Closing my eyes again, I wondered if he was waiting on someone else. Taking a deep breath, I put out a thought out to Spirit. *Help me.* Concentrating on my clairvoyance, I could see a bullmastiff dog.

He is going to think I have truly lost the plot; talking to animals now.

However, I trusted my vision.

"This may sound a little odd – I rarely connect to animals in Spirit but there is a dog here. It's a bullmastiff. He's white and has a black patch over his eye. He's not long passed over and had to be put to sleep. His back legs had gone and it was the best decision to stop his suffering."

The man, who previously had such a tough exterior, suddenly broke down crying.

"That's my dog," he said through tears. "I had to have him put down last week. I'm heartbroken."

Looking at this broken man with sympathy, I reassured him: "I feel your dog wants you to know he's okay. I sense a great freedom; he's no longer in pain. He really was a best friend to you in many ways."

"I feel your parents are asking you to let go of guilt," I went on. "You made a loving choice for him."

I did my best to comfort him, but little did I know I'd be facing the same heartache a few months later.

My big ginger cat Tom, who I'd owned for seven years, was showing signs of poor health. He was tired all the time, losing weight and wasn't eating. The vets took his bloods and kept him in overnight.

On the drive home from the vets, I had a terrible feeling.

Spirit, is Tom going to die?

"Yes." I heard it clearly. Pulling the car over, I broke down crying. I knew it.

The vet rang the following morning to share the distressing news.

"Angela, I'm really sorry to tell you this," the vet began gently. "Tom's bloods have come back. He has a rare form of blood cancer; Leukaemia. It's best that we put him to sleep."

I felt terrible. *Why hadn't I brought him earlier and got him checked?*

Maybe I could bring him home and give him heal-

ing? I thought optimistically. But realistically, I knew I couldn't save him. It was just his time. Time to let go peacefully.

I drove to the vets to say goodbye; with mum coming along for moral support. I worried it would be too distressing for Gabrielle so I thought it best to leave her with my sister.

Tom was doped up with medication and looked so tired. I knew his wee soul was already going. I just wanted to take him home; to cuddle and care for him. Crying, I told him how much he meant to me and how much I loved him. As they gave him his final injection, my emotions poured out and I sobbed goodbye.

We left the vets, our hearts broken. They had given me Tom's remains, carefully wrapped up. We decided to bury him in our backyard. Digging a hole for him was next to impossible; I had to keep stopping to wipe my tears away. We laid our beautiful cat gently into the ground, saying a prayer. Gabrielle and I stood silently, holding each together and looking at the muddy earth.

Consoling one another, we both became aware of a distinct smell in the air.

"Can you smell that?" I asked Gabrielle.

"Yes, mummy," she responded, red-eyed.

"That's Tom's smell." The aroma lingered for about a minute, then faded. I knew he was giving us a sign; to let us know his soul was at peace.

I had a similar experience when my dog Scruffy passed away. I didn't understand it at the time, but I do now. Spirit communicates through various signs; one of which is smell.

The signs didn't stop there. A few months after Tom's passing, I found a large clump of ginger hair sitting neatly on the hallway mat. I picked up the fluffy fur and started laughing. It was his way of saying: *"Hello!"*

I was still itching for a new work premises when my sister announced her office space no longer felt right for her. She asked if I'd like to take it on and I jumped at the chance. It was on the Falls Road, Belfast; just as my guide *Chi* had shown me in meditation.

I opened a mind and body shop called *House of Healing.* This was the centre that Spirit wanted me teach and demonstrate from.

The guidance from meditation was finally falling into place.

I was buzzing with excitement; my very own shop and holistic centre! As soon as I settled in, I was inundated with requests. It was a busy time;

private sittings; a circle to teach others and workshops. The DJ work had to be put on a backburner while I devoted time to mediumship.

Aware of the huge responsibility that came with personal readings and recognising the growing expectations, I really wanted to educate myself further. I attended the Arthur Findlay College in London several times a year, keen to enhance my abilities.

There were courses for mediumship, healing, art and trance – I loved it! There was so much diversity and I met individuals from all around the world. The energy was amazing and it was a joy listening to a host of wonderful teachers.

At the college, I kept getting the same message from different mediums:

You will be a platform worker for Spirit.

That would mean going up on stage in front of audiences! I would bring information from loved ones passed to Spirit; evidence that we don't die, our souls live on.

A short time after opening my shop, I made another bold move. I began to organise "Evenings of Mediumship". I booked hotels and theatres and arranged guest mediums. Tickets sold out within minutes. It was a positive sign from Spirit that it was meant to be. I was learning to trust the guidance.

Preparing myself for a demonstration of mediumship later that evening, I had just finished getting my hair blow-dried. Glancing at my watch, I noticed the time: *4pm.*

I better eat something before work.

I wanted a late lunch with my sisters but no one was available. Deciding to try out a local restaurant, I happily took a seat on my own.

A lovely blonde-haired waitress came over and handed me a menu.

"Hello, would you like a drink?"

"Yes please, some water and lemon thanks."

Eyeing me up and down, she observed, "You're that medium, Angela, aren't you?"

"Erm, yes I am," I murmured, feeling slightly embarrassed. I didn't recognise the waitress and knew we'd never met.

"I'd love to go to one," she admitted, looking at me with curiosity.

"Oh really?"

"Yes, it frightens me a little. I've never been to a medium before," she confided. "I'd be afraid if the person I wanted to connect with, didn't come through."

"If you do go for a reading, it's best to keep an open mind. It's a healing experience for many people," I advised, trying to keep the conversation light and breezy.

I could feel the energy change around us and I knew Spirit was present. I didn't say anything about it. I just scanned the menu quickly and rattled off my order.

I waited patiently on my food, enjoying people watching, but my attention kept going back to the waitress.

I could feel spirit, but I held back from telling her. I was unsure if it was the person she wanted and I didn't know how she'd react.

My food arrived and the waitress passed by to check on me.

"Everything ok?"

"Yes, it's lovely." Every time I looked at her, I knew spirit wanted to pass on a message.

Finishing my meal and going up to the counter to pay, the waitress handed me the bill.

"Hope everything was okay for you."

"It was great thanks," I replied. "Listen, you do have someone from Spirit with you," I admitted nervously. "Would you like me to pass on the message?"

Her face dropped in surprise. "Yes! Of course!"

"Your daddy is here, along with your mum's mummy. Your dad wants me to tell you that the fluid problems he had with his lung and chest have now all cleared. He has put weight back on and is still wearing his flat cap."

Her eyes welled up with tears.

"He loved your mum and family deeply. You were a daddy's girl. He's giving me the names Jim and Patrick."

Astonished, she confirmed, "Jim is my daddy's name and Patrick was his father. My daddy died with lung cancer."

"He knows about the baby boy about to be born," I continued.

Crying, she confirmed her daughter was days away from giving birth and they found out it was a boy.

"Your daddy knows his name, James, will be passed onto your new grandson."

"Yes, that's right," she confirmed. "My daughter is going to give him James as a middle name."

"Tell your mummy and the family that he loves you all deeply and he is okay. That's his biggest message," I concluded, feeling the contact grow fainter.

Smiling, she gave me a big hug and thanked me for her first ever reading.

I didn't go to dinner that night with the intention of communicating with spirit. I only wanted a peaceful meal, but Spirit had other plans!

I was delighted to bring comfort and reassurance from her father. Spirit brings the magic; mediums get the joy of passing it on.

CHAPTER TWELVE

Joby Murphy

"DA, CAN YOU give me a lift to work?" Joby called downstairs.

"Yes son, just let me know when you're ready to go," Joe chirped back.

Joe, a single dad to Joby, Stacey, Kevin and Martin, didn't always find life easy. Juggling work and bills, Joe did his best to provide for his kids. A devoted dad, Joe's joinery work just about covered the costs of family life.

Joby was a twenty-year-old lad, laid-back and fun-loving. He loved playing rugby and easily made friends. He loved travelling, especially to Canada. The family had friends there and he'd been flying back and forth from a young age. It was a dream of his to one day live abroad.

Getting dressed in his work clothes, Joby also packed a fresh shirt and jeans in a rucksack. He'd be going to a concert later that night with his girlfriend.

Joe and Joby, who had a great relationship, lapsed into their usual light banter as they made the short journey to Belfast city centre. Joe worried about all of his children, but especially Joby. Being an adventurous twenty-year-old, Joby thought he could handle a drink and sometimes went overboard.

It didn't help that the club Joby would be going to after work, sold shots of vodka at only one pound. Being the protective father, Joe tried to warn his son. "Joby, be careful tonight. Stay away from those shots."

Joby laughed it off, trying to downplay his dad's worries. Pulling up outside Joby's work, Joe wished him well.

"Look after yourself, have a good night."

Little did Joe know, that would be the last conversation he would ever have with his son.

The next day Joe didn't hear from Joby. This wasn't entirely unusual as Joby spent a lot of time at his girlfriend's house. Knowing that Joby had been to a concert the night before, Joby assumed he was probably tired and relaxing with his girlfriend.

A few days passed however and still no word. Starting to worry, Joe knew in his gut something was wrong.

On phoning Joby's girlfriend, it turned out she was thinking the same thing. She hadn't seen him for a few days either and assumed he was at home with his dad.

She relayed the events of the night out. After the concert, they went on to a nightclub. Joby drank four or five double vodkas. Concerned he was too drunk, she decided it was time they went home. She took him outside to get a taxi but Joby insisted he wanted to stay out. He said he'd follow her home later. Reluctantly, she agreed.

Joby's brothers, Martin and Kevin, began phoning around Joby's mates, trying to find out who he could be staying with. No-one knew where he was.

It was time to phone the police.

The police noted all the details and told them they'd be in touch as soon as they had more information.

The following day, a police car pulled up outside Joe's home. Two policemen got out and began walking up the garden path. Joe's stomach flipped; he knew it wasn't good news. Hearing their firm knocks, Joe approached the front door, shaking with nerves.

"Yes?"

"Can we come in? We have some news about your son Joby."

Terrified, Joe invited them in.

Sitting down with Joe, the police explained they scanned through the CCTV. They observed Joby and his girlfriend leaving the concert and going into the adjacent nightclub.

Joby could be seen at the bar, downing the cheap vodka shots that Joe warned him about.

The video footage showed Joby staggering outside onto a foot-bridge at Belfast Harbour. Hovering over the water, he lost his footing, slipped accidentally and plummeted into the river below.

The police were unsure if he had drowned or if he had swum away to safety.

Joe felt in his heart that Joby was dead. However, he didn't want to trust his intuition; he wanted to find his son. They had to get him home. That was the main focus now; nothing else mattered.

Get Joby home.

Over the next few weeks, friends and local community members pulled together to help in the search for Joby. During daylight hours, the family stood by the riverside watching helplessly as police divers looked for his body. The freezing, wet, January weather didn't deter their lingering – they waited anxiously, desperate for any news.

Joe longed for his boy back and the family wanted their beautiful brother. Local residents came out in droves, yearning to help with this tragic disappearance. Candlelit vigils of prayer were held, with members of the community coming along to offer their support.

The news was relayed widely in the local press. Joe was hearing reports that his son had *jumped* into the water, not slipped. The implication of suicide angered and distressed him. He knew that his son loved life; that this was nothing short of a tragic accident.

Joe took the opportunity to contact local newspapers. He was able to use the press to run front page articles, appealing for Joby's return. Not only was he able to question his son's whereabouts, he was also able to highlight the danger of promotional cheap alcohol.

"Young people don't realise the strength of these drinks. They buy cheap vodka and believe they can get away with double doses. They're think they're only out to have a good time. They have no idea it can kill. Something has to be done to stop it. We have to protect our youngsters," Joe warned. His only hope was that was his words of advice would stop another family going through what he was suffering.

Two weeks later, the search had come to nothing. Joe was told that the tide had probably washed Joby's body out to sea.

But still, Joe didn't give up.

Along with his family, Joe took a boat out himself, searching around Belfast Lough and Carrickfergus. The wintry conditions put them at risk, but they were desperate to find Joby's body; to bring him home.

It was all to no avail. Joby was still missing.

Whether it was desperation or divine timing, Joe's godson spotted an advert for my Evening of Mediumship.

Thinking it was a good idea, John suggested it to the family; "She might know where Joby is. What have we got to lose?"

Deciding to give it a go, John bought three tickets. Joe had never attended a medium before and had no idea if it would help.

Alongside my Evenings of Mediumship in theatres and hotels, I also began holding smaller group sessions. I would deliver messages and guidance from loved ones who had passed to Spirit. These took place in my centre, House of Healing. Only sixteen people could fit in one room, making it a more intimate experience.

On a cold, dull, winter Wednesday night, sixteen strangers entered the building. There were three rows of chairs laid out for them and my mum showed the attendees to their seats.

I was waiting in another room, preparing to greet my guests and hoping I would be of service to those eagerly waiting.

There's a build-up of nerves before every demonstration. I've come to realise this is a natural surge of adrenaline. Glancing at my watch, I saw that it was almost eight o'clock. Time to start. Making my way into the room, the conversation hushed to a stop. I introduced myself and told them a little about what they might expect from the evening.

"I work as medium and I hope to communicate with your loved ones. They may wish to share evidence of their lives and relay their memories of you. They may also wish to offer guidance. Please keep an open mind."

Glancing around the room, I noticed three

men sitting in the back row together; one older man and two younger lads. I recognised the older man from the newspapers. I knew Joe had been appealing to the public about his son.

Apprehensively, I knew that he was looking for some miraculous message of Joby's whereabouts. We had never met before, and yet I felt compelled to offer some compassionate words of hope or guidance.

Despite anticipating their expectations, I began my mediumship and, as always, had learned to trust my impressions.

Immediately, I could feel a mother; I knew she was for Joe.

"May I work with you," I began.

Shocked, he sat up straight in his chair. "Yes love," he looked at me with his piercing blue eyes.

"I have your mother here. She's a small, feisty woman with an apron around her waist; thin build. She had a large family and she's giving me the name Jean."

Filling up with tears, he blurted out; "Yes, my mum's name is Jean! And yes, that fits her description."

"She's giving me ten in the family and I can

see the Ardoyne area," I told him.

"Yes, there's eight children and then my mum and dad. We grew up in Ardoyne," he confirmed.

The energy from his mother Jean was very strong. I began rubbing around my tummy area. "Your mum had problems with her lower stomach; the women's area," I observed.

"Yeah, mum had cancer in that area. She had to have a hysterectomy. They gave her the all-clear, but they hadn't got some of the cancer out. That's how she died," he advised.

The energy around me began to change. My awareness of Jean was still present but I knew she was bringing her grandson forward.

"Your mummy is telling me she has Joby with her in Spirit. I can feel your son now standing beside me."

Gasping, Joe's mouth fell open.

"Joby says it was an accident," I stated. "He wants you to know you're looking in the wrong area for him."

The audience members looked on in stunned silence as Joby explained his whereabouts.

"Joby's body is still in the harbour. He's not out at sea. You'll find him towards the left side of the harbour. There's a life buoy on the wall. His leg is caught on machinery and he's under a boat. That's where you'll find him."

"He's keeps saying you'll find him on the day of the big search," I said, trusting the information I was receiving, even if I didn't fully understand it.

Joe was astonished at what I was relaying and to be honest, so was I. I didn't expect his son to show me the exact whereabouts of his body, but I've learned to be fully trusting of Spirit. I hoped with all my heart that this message would help them find him. Maybe then, the family could finally lay Joby to rest.

"He's a lovely fella," I continued. "I know you were all very close to him. He sends his love to you and the family. He loves you all so much."

When the evening drew to a close, Joe and his sons came up to me at the end and thanked me for the message. They were able to confirm all the evidence from his mother Jean, but they couldn't confirm Joby's; not until he was found. Not yet.

My heart went out for Joe and his family. It was difficult to deliver news about the whereabouts of Joby's dead body, especially when they were still clinging on to the hope that he was alive.

A few weeks later, Joe informed me that the Community Rescue Service launched a massive search and rescue event. Alongside Mallow Search and Rescue, they used high-tech sonar equipment to search for Joby.

Joe told them to check the area I had mentioned. Using their sonar equipment, they scanned the entire harbour area. It was 25th February 2012; 31 days after Joby went missing. This was the *'big search'* that Joby had talked about in the reading.

Joby's body was found on the left-hand side of the harbour. He was underneath a boat, next to a lifebuoy hanging on the wall. It was the exact same spot he had accurately described in the reading.

A coroner ruled that his death had been accidental; a likely result of alcohol and cold weather. After months of confusion and uncertainty, the family were finally able to lay Joby to rest. Slowly beginning the grieving process, they could pay their respects at his funeral and give him the send-off he deserved.

A few months later, Joe and his family launched the 'Joby Murphy Trust'. The intention was to turn their hardship into helping others.

They had to wait weeks for sonar equipment, so they wanted to raise money to purchase this life-saving kit for others. Joe's family raised a staggering £45,000. The much-needed hi-tech machinery has reduced the waiting time for many other families.

Joby's soul understood the importance of passing on a message to his father and brothers. With sheer determination, he was able to verify his eternal existence. I believe Joby and Jean truly helped their family to realise they'd always be with them. They wanted to bring them peace and comfort in their time of need.

No soul is ever lost, even in tragedy.

CHAPTER THIRTEEN

House of Healing

MY SHOP *HOUSE of Healing,* was doing so well that I decided to relocate to Belfast city centre. The greater footfall would give me an opportunity to connect with more clients. Setting up the shop and preparing to welcome new clients gave me immense joy. It felt like a world away from when I first started out, working from the kitchen table in my humble flat.

Our premises was now on three floors. We had a new age shop on the ground floor, selling everything from crystals and jewellery to books and oracle cards. Upstairs, we had cosy rooms for readings and healing. We were also very fortunate to have a skilled Shamanic practitioner, healer and medium working alongside us: Richard Martin.

I had finished off my readings for the day with a man in his early sixties. Many of his family had come forward to communicate with him, including his wife and parents. I knew he had been feeling lonely for years, so I was glad to see that the reading settled him. He knew that his loved ones were with him.

After the session, I asked if I could give him a hug. It wasn't uncommon for me to offer a hug after working with someone. It's such a personal experience and it's a huge privilege to link with their loved ones in Spirit. A hug is a lovely way to end a private sitting.

Uncomfortably, he agreed. I hugged him for a few seconds and thanked him for allowing me to read for him.

"You know something," he began, tears in his eyes. "I've not had a hug in years."

Compassion and love oozing towards him, I chirped, "Well, I'm going to give you another hug in that case!" I reached over and gave him a massive squeeze.

Laughing and blushing, he thanked me and began walking downstairs. I felt uplifted from such a small interaction. As the lovely gentleman left the shop, I walked over to the window and watched the hurried shoppers passing by. Christmas was fast approaching and the dark evenings had settled in. The ground was soaked with rain and people scurried by, under cover of hoods and umbrellas.

I couldn't help but notice the low mood. People seemed apprehensive and uptight, perhaps worrying about money and Christmas. The longer I observed the shoppers, I began to see Spirit people. Every individual who walked along the street was followed by a loved one in Spirit. Focusing on one lady, I noticed her mother in spirit behind her. The daughter looked so overwhelmed and anxious. Her mother was trying to reassure her; to lift her mood from her anxious thoughts. Her mum loved her so much and was trying her best to communicate. The daughter seemed completely unaware, but I knew her mother would get her attention at some point.

When we worry or feel overwhelmed, the Spirit world wants to reach out. This experience was a reminder that Spirit is always trying to help. We have loved ones with us any time we need them. They love us unconditionally.

✧   ✧   ✧

THE ATMOSPHERE OF my *House of Healing* shop provided a warm welcome to clients. Normally, people were very nervous when they arrived. However, when the reading was over and they were leaving, you could visibly notice their faces relax.

Fortunately, my mum worked alongside me every day. Her loving and compassionate nature was a great source of comfort for people, both before and after their reading. Sometimes individuals came out of the reading, emotional, with tears in their eyes. We were always on hand to offer kindness in the form of a cup of tea, a hankie or a hug! People just needed to be listened to and understood. Readings gave them the reassurance that loved ones are with them in Spirit.

You are not alone.

I was proud of the space I had created for people. I loved the warm environment that we had provided for healing. The centre was unique in that way. When people came into the shop, they were looking for comfort; a place to unwind and talk about their struggles. Even if they just came in to browse, my mum would always end up listening to their stories. People felt comfortable to open up to her and have a cry. It was a healing shop filled with compassion for anyone who wished to use it.

I got stuck into what I love most; sharing my insights through private readings, teaching and demonstrating. This was my life now and I was grateful for it. At times though, I still had niggling moments of doubt. Thoughts of uncertainty tried to creep in. However, I trusted implicitly in Spirit's direction for me. Even today, I still choose to listen to my inner nudges; my gut feeling, my intuitive ideas. Experience has taught me to let go and have faith.

When mum wasn't working, we were lucky to have another worker called Tracey helping us out. Tracey and I always had a lot of fun, laughter and banter together. When Tracey first started working at the shop, she used to worry that I could read her mind! Jokingly, I would play along with her and pretend that I could, just to freak her out. However, she quickly learned that I am as normal and down-to-earth as the next person, and I certainly can't read minds!

When we finished up at work one day, I offered to give Tracey a lift home. As we drove in the direction of her house, I unfortunately had a sudden overwhelming feeling that one of her boys had been hurt.

"Tracey, I don't mean to freak you out, but I

saw something there," I said, trying to keep the anxiety out of my voice.

"What? What did you see?" Tracey looked out of the window, trying to follow my line of vision.

"No, I mean I saw a psychic image in my mind. I can see one of your boys being brought to hospital," I kept my tone as calm and sensitive as I could.

"What?" Tracey looked at me, alarmed. I had never spoken to her like this before and I'm sure she didn't know what way to take me.

"I can see one of your boys; I'm unsure which one, but his arm is injured. It's his lower left arm. You'll need to take him to hospital to make sure a doctor looks at it."

"What? What do you mean?" Tracey, who was a worrier at the best of times, now looked petrified.

"Don't worry," I assured her. "His arm will be fine, but just make sure you take him to hospital to get it checked out."

Looking aghast, she opened the car door and rushed out to check on him. "Okay!" she called. "I'll let you know!"

Arriving inside, Tracey noticed a pool of blood in her hallway. Thinking the worst, she cried out: "Hello! Who's in? What's happened? What's going on?"

No-one was home.

Frantic, Tracey ran up the street to her mother-in-law's.

Opening the door, she saw Reece, her youngest son, with his left arm wrapped in a towel. A dog had bitten him. Tracey rushed him to casualty. The doctor told him that he was a very lucky boy; that the dog could have bitten off his entire arm. Thankfully, he only suffered puncture wounds. His arm was thoroughly cleaned and bandaged.

The psychic visions kept coming for the people I worked with. I had found my passion and loved every moment working for Spirit. I wanted people to know the truth I experienced every day; that we have Spirit's guidance when we need it. They love us and only want to be of service.

THE SHOP WAS always full of activity which was wonderful, but I needed a little break to switch off and relax. Arranging to meet a friend in Edinburgh, I boarded the plane for a short flight to Scotland. I had a strange feeling this wouldn't be an ordinary flight.

It was small plane of around eighty seats. As it began filling up, no-one sat beside me. I had a feeling Spirit was scheming something, but I wasn't sure yet. The last passenger boarded the plane. She was dressed in a pilot's uniform, but instead of going into the cockpit, she approached the empty seat next to me.

As she sat down, I smiled at her and we exchanged pleasantries. Glancing out the window, I settled into my seat as the plane began its upward journey.

I'd never met a real-life pilot before and was curious about her career, but I wasn't sure if she wanted to chat or to sit in silence.

Testing the waters, I threw out the question: "So, have you been a pilot long?"

Thankfully, she seemed open to having a polite conversation.

"Yes, I've been working for years as a pilot," she told me, and continued to openly chat about her job. As the conversation flowed easily, I suddenly became aware of her father in Spirit standing beside her in the aisle.

I knew her father wanted to pass on a message, but I wasn't sure how I could bring it into the conversation. *How am I going to tell her? She'll think she's sitting next to some looney!*

I didn't mention anything about her father during the entire flight. However, as the plane touched down towards landing, I knew her dad might never get the chance to communicate with her again. Building up my courage, I reminded myself that even if she thought I was loopy, the chances of ever bumping into her again were very slim.

"I work as a medium," I told her, finding an opportunity to drop it into the conversation.

"Oh? What's that then?" she enquired in her soft Scottish accent.

Oh my goodness, she doesn't even know what a medium is! She's going to think I'm crazy!

"I communicate with loved ones that have passed over," I explained, trying to sound calmer than I felt.

To my horror, she screwed her face up. This was a look I had seen before. It was a look of disbelief and incredulity; a look that told me she thought I was nuts.

"I know this sounds a little weird, but your father is standing next to you. Can I pass on a message from him?"

Now she was intrigued. She looked at me curiously and, without saying a word, nodded.

"He's giving me the name Jim. He's talking about memories of living in the countryside. You must have grown up on a farm. I feel that was his job."

Her eyes welled up. "Yes, my father's name is James, he was known as Jim. We lived on a farm."

The plane had landed by now, seatbelts were clicking off and passengers were restlessly eager to retrieve their overhead baggage.

However, I sat calmly and continued with her father's message. "Don't worry too much about your marriage," I soothed. "Everyone has ups and downs. It will get better. You've just got to work at communicating with each other; making more time for each other."

People were standing up, shuffling about, collecting their belongings and moving down the aisle, while I continued relaying her father's message.

"I know your dad was a very private man, but I feel he loved you deeply. He wants you to know he is still with you."

Tears sprang to her eyes as she wiped them

away quickly. An air hostess approached us, eyeing me suspiciously.

"Is everything okay here?" she asked.

"It's grand," the pilot smiled bravely. "It's all okay."

I don't normally pass messages on to strangers I've just met, especially strangers who haven't requested a reading!

I got off the plane that day and never bumped into that pilot again. However, I felt assured that I had passed on the father's request. When we parted ways, she had thanked me for the reassurance I gave her.

At least now she knows her father is still around and watching over her.

CHAPTER FOURTEEN

The Soul

MOST OF THE individuals that come to me are worried about loved ones who have passed. They are seeking answers to many different questions:

- *Are they okay? Are they safe? Are they still with me? What is the Spirit world?*
- *Are they still with me? How can I experience them as you do?*
- *Why don't I dream of them like other family members do?*
- *Can they give me signs?*
- *Will they ever leave me? Did I do something to cause their passing?*
- *Could I have done more to help them? Do they know how much I love them?*
- *Do they know I am sorry?*

Those who experience a reading can get some answers to these questions. They can finally have some clarity and heal from internal conflicts they may have. Readings are positive and uplifting; they are a useful guide to help us through difficult times.

Experiencing a reading can help to settle uncomfortable feelings of:–

- remorse, resentment, anger, bitterness, upset, a negative mindset,
- doubt, grief, frustration, uncertainty, concern, confusion, sadness.

God wants us to know that the consciousness of the soul lives on. Mediums wouldn't exist if this wasn't the case. God is the Spirit of life; the soul is the expression from Spirit. The soul has the desire to prove its eternal existence.

The soul is the individualised part of God that makes us unique. The talents, gifts and attributes that we are born with, are brought to earth to be expressed through the Spirit. The Spirit is God. It's in everything; every animal, plant, mineral. It's life itself. Our soul uses Spirit to express our individualism.

Our souls live on; our consciousness, our memories. We meet loved ones discarnate. We are Spiritual beings. We have a resource of love and knowledge within. Your soul is a wise counsellor. To embrace and get to know your soul, you need to learn to sit and be present. Meditation can be a great aid to access your inner guide.

At times, we lose sight of what's important in life. We can focus too much on material things. We might be prone to overthinking, fear and anxiety. The external world around us can lead us away from Spiritualising ourselves. We need to slow down. We can learn to relax through breath-work; to be still and quieten the mind. We have an internal world within us. It's an abundant source of help. The practice of meditation and prayer can help you get to know your own soul. It can bring about a change in your perspective and personality.

Regular meditation can instil a deep sense of calm and peace of mind. It will ground you in the present moment. You may react to your thoughts, feelings and situations differently. As you learn to tune into your soul, your mind is less likely to be overwhelmed by negative, anxious or stressful feelings. You will learn to trust in yourself, going more with the flow and accepting situations that arise. Meditating can create a positive impact on your relationships. As you learn to quieten your mind, you will find greater balance.

During meditation, you may be inspired with creative solutions to difficulties. At times, you may experience visions to help your life's purpose. Your sleep patterns will improve. Fatigue and depression will reduce as a result of meditating regularly.

Life is forever changing. External circumstances can be challenging at times. Getting in touch with your soul is the only true and lasting source of happiness. Going within means that you no longer need to depend on outer conditions to fulfil you. People and material possessions can add to your life. They will come and go, but a Spiritual power will sustain you. As you feel this power of love and healing flow through you, you will be nourished by its love. To feel at home. To be at peace. To feel connected to all of life.

Meditation is truly a wonderful support to your overall well-being. You only need to sit for a few moments each day, practising breathing in and breathing out with your eyes closed.

When a loved one dies, he or she continues to have cognitive experiences even after death. The departed soul has reason, emotion and desire within. The soul retains memories of physical life and has a desire to communicate and help us.

When a loved one from Spirit blends with me, that individual soul is making a choice to communicate. It's never forced. The soul passed has an intention. He or she has an urge, a desire; a need to prove they are safe and well.

They know where their loved ones are. When I give an *Evening of Mediumship* at a theatre, the soul knows the time and place of the event. They know where their loved one is seated in the audience. It proves the soul's intelligence. People in spirit have no physical eyes or ears, but they can sense. They hear, see and feel using their Spiritual senses.

Spirit wants to demystify our fear of death. Loved ones passed seek to comfort us in our time of distress. They need us to know that they are safe and happy. The Spirit world is an atmosphere free from pain; emotional, mental and physical. There is no illness. The soul is unrestricted from the limitations of old thinking patterns. They are in a feeling place of freedom and joy. They are energised, vibrant and refreshed. They have insight and awareness into our lives; the ability to see our gifts and potential.

They love us and want to positively influence

our lives. Loved ones who have passed will always encourage us through every stage of our lives. They have an awareness of changes that have taken place since they passed over. They want to reassure us they are no longer in pain. The soul doesn't feel pain. We do. They are conscious of their environment and us. Mediumship invites us to be open to the idea that Spirit exists alongside us. Our loved ones passed are eternal beings. Their love and support are only a thought away.

Mediumship demonstrates to us that we are never without Spirit's help. It can help to renew our faith, gives us hope and brings peace. Loved ones passed want to comfort their family and friends in their time of grief. Souls deceased want to console those that need them. They long to bring peace to their loved one; to reassure those who feel lost, confused or hurt. Mediumship relieves both the soul departed and those living. It joins two people together; reuniting each other in love, reminding us that we're never alone in dealing with life's struggles.

I remember doing a reading from a grandmother in Spirit who was communicating to her grand-daughter. During the reading, the granny showed me a vision of her last moments upon her death.

"Your grandmother is giving me a vision of lying on the hospital bed after she died. She was above her body, looking down. She had the awareness that she was no longer in her body, and yet, she was still conscious of her surroundings. She knew she had died."

"She wants to let you know that she felt freer than she has ever felt. No more physical illness or mental worry. She's describing her death as though it was just like taking off a coat."

When someone is very ill and about to die, deceased people in Spirit will sometimes be present beside them. The dying person tells their family that they have had a visitation. They know that family members are waiting for them on the other side. They aren't delusional. So many have had this experience. Spirit are preparing them to make the transition.

When a loved one passes, they are greeted by deceased family members, angels and guides. No one is left on their own. Everyone has Spiritual helpers guiding their transition back into the Spirit world. Some souls quickly readjust to their surroundings; others may take a little longer.

When they pass over, all souls will become aware they're no longer in a physical body. They are still conscious.

Having this new awareness, they have choices:-

They can recreate any experience they wish. Angels and guides will be present for all souls at every stage. When the soul is ready, they can change their experience as quickly as they think it to be. All souls will be embraced by the purest essence of God's love and energy.

The soul has a completely new perspective when they cross over. They get to know their true self. They have choices, just as we do. They go through a period of reflection. Each soul gets to experience every thought, action and word they shared. The soul comes to understand how their words and actions may have impacted someone. This isn't from a place of judgement, but one of observation. From this new awareness, the soul has a different insight into the life they lived.

When souls connect with a medium, they sometimes use it as a healing experience for both the sitter and themselves. They apologise for hurt they may have caused to loved ones.

At one of my demonstrations, a father from

Spirit went direct to his daughter. I could feel the father's remorse immediately. He was sorry for not being present in his daughter's life.

"I have your father from Spirit here. He was only fifty-four when he died, is that correct?"

"Yes," she nodded.

"You loved your daddy but there were emotional issues between you. He lost himself in drinking. This had a huge impact on your family. Your dad is showing me he left your mum when you were young. He's saying he wasn't in your life after this. Does that make sense?"

Crying, she nodded in agreement.

"He's deeply sorry for being absent. You were angry with him for a long time. You'd ask why he didn't come to see you; why he didn't make an effort. He did try at times but you were frustrated by his attitude; his arrogance and self-importance."

She agreed with all I was sharing. I continued on, offering her his healing words:

"Your inner child needed this tonight. Your daddy does love you, but the drink destroyed him. He couldn't express his love back then, but now that he's in Spirit, he can."

"He's talking about when he was found dead.

He doesn't want you replaying that vision in your mind any longer. He asks you to please stop worrying about his passing. Does this relate?"

"Yes, my daddy was found," she shared, wiping away a tear.

"He says he passed quickly and didn't experience any pain. He feels well in Spirit; complete."

"The relationship with your dad was fractured and unfortunately you don't have great memories to look back on. However, he wants you to know that he loves you and you are important to him. You're not on your own."

"He knows you have forgiven him. You're not holding on to that hurt or anger anymore. You can look back and have compassion and understanding for him. He's so proud of you."

Bringing the contact to a close, I let her know: "He is safe and well in Spirit."

In Spirit, the dad took the opportunity to apologize to his daughter and express his love for her. He was able to have a clear understanding of the impact of his words and actions. He knew exactly where she was sitting in the audience. He could sense how her memories were affecting her emotionally. He was able to heal her fears surrounding his death. He had the ability to relieve her anxiety by letting her know he was well and happy in Spirit.

Her dad had the awareness that she had forgiven him. He showed me that by giving me evidence of their relationship. He proved that his soul had survived and that he was still consciously with her. His love for her was all that mattered.

Souls who pass suddenly or tragically will be reunited with family and friends who have passed already. Every soul who dies is given help to settle into their new surroundings. They are okay; they're in a place of peace – we need not worry. Spirit wants to reassure; to help us experience the same peace they are feeling.

If someone has died unexpectedly and they connect through me to you, they will do their best to bring hope and reassurance. Why? Because you are so deeply loved; you are important to them. You are their focus. They want peace for your life.

Sometimes, Spirit is keen to share insight into their loved one's future. They want to encourage that positive, joyful times are ahead.

A young girl, early twenties, came to me for a personal reading. As soon as the reading began, I became aware of her boyfriend in Spirit. He had passed away only a few months before. He showed me he had died in a car accident. She found out she pregnant around the time of the accident. Understandingly, she was distraught; six months pregnant and grieving the loss of her beloved partner.

During the reading, the boyfriend showed me that the baby would grow up with a step-dad. He told his partner that she would get married and go on to have more children. Naturally, she didn't want to hear any such thing; so overwhelmed she was with her loss. She didn't believe the news and only wanted to be with him. I told her there'd be a few tough years ahead, but her boyfriend wanted to help secure a better future for them.

He reassured her that he'd always be there as a father for their child, but that he wanted a secure life for her and the child. His desire to communicate this emanated from his soul's love.

A few years after the reading, she came back for another. Smiling, she told me she had got engaged to a new partner. She let me that both her and her child were very happy. Her partner in spirit was able to see clearly what she couldn't.

His promise was true.

✧　✧　✧

LOVED ONES WHO have passed away decades before will continue to watch over the lives of their family. Because they are no longer in the physical world, we assume they aren't around to watch their children or grand-children grow up. This is not the case. There have been many examples where passed loved ones have validated their continued presence to me.

Take the time I was doing a demonstration in a hotel.

The room had filled up to maximum capacity with only two seats vacant. I noticed two women, early thirties, squeezing into the remaining two chairs at the back of the room. I also realised I had a father from Spirit wanting to connect to one of the girls.

Picking her out of the crowd, I asked if she was okay to receive a communication.

"Yes," she blushed, pulling her scarf over her mouth to hide her face.

"Your father is passed, is that correct?"

"Yes," she confirmed, surprised.

"He's telling me he passed when you were a young child. You may have very vague memories of him, but he's been with you all of your life."

Her eyes glistening, she seemed touched with this revelation.

"You have a son, don't you?" I asked. I could feel her father's interest in the grandson he never got to meet.

"Yes, I have a son," she confirmed.

"Your dad knows his passion for football. He's an incredibly talented young boy. Your dad's telling me that footballing scouts have noticed him at the club. He's so passionate about the sport, isn't he?"

Crying and laughing at the same time, she could hardly believe what I was saying.

"Yes, my little boy is in a team and scouts have been over to watch him play," she told us.

"Please know that your father watches over him. The boy – is he about six or seven?"

"He's seven."

"I think it's wonderful evidence. It shows that your dad has always been with you, and will always be with you. He's encouraging your son with the football. He feels he'll go far with it."

Her dad proved that he was aware of his daughter's son and the boy's interests. His love for both of them was very apparent.

Spirit will always positively affect our lives – we just need to have faith they are helping us. Spirit is guiding you always. Let go of worries, fears and anxieties. You're not on your own.

Remember those deceased have a soul. A medium communicates with this non-physical essence, the cumulation of collective memories we have experienced in life. Our soul's core is the life force of God's divinity encompassed within it.

Each of us have our own soul. By taking the time to connect with our inner being through practices of meditation and prayer you will see miracles unfolding and manifesting in your life. Your soul will give you the intuitive ideas and indications to your purpose. Getting closer to your soul means getting closer to God. You will understand what really matters, you will use your time more wisely, focus on creating a life of meaning and service to others.

If you seek peace, insight or guidance, learn to be still. If you seek direction, purpose, love or connection, learn to be still. Practice, one day a time, opening yourself up to the Power that is all around you. Invite its presence to blend with you. Allow God's energy to restore you back to balance. Some find it helpful to join a class or to access guided meditations online. Making the effort will re-energise you. Being present in your soul is giving yourself a gift of love.

MIRACLE STORIES

Miracles are Real

I BELIEVE MY calling is to serve others as a Spiritual Medium. The synchronicity of people and places were aligned in divine timing for my soul to manifest my purpose. There were no accidents with the individuals and environments that led me towards my path into the world of mediumship. Belonging to a family with generational mediumistic ability was my first stepping stone to the indication that I also have this gift. I may not have known this during my younger years, but I have come to realise I was being guided by a mystical power to serve others.

When I first got involved in mediumship, it challenged my mindset; that there is no death, that our souls live on, that I was able to blend with a soul who is deceased and pass on their memories and message. I had to examine what I believed to be impossible; to move beyond the limitations of the mind. I had to open myself up to the possibility that the Spirit world could work through me; to understand that God's power was making this a reality for those I came into contact with.

I had to go beyond my rational mind and real-ise that Spirit has nothing to do with logic. When I work, I am tapping into a spiritual realm of consciousness; an eternity of memories from souls passed. I have faith that Spirit's power exists around us at all times. When the conditions are right, mediumship is able to manifest.

I have come to the realisation that medi-umship is a mystical experience and manifests as a miracle for those I work with. It occurs as a natural, spontaneous phenomena. I can never guarantee the outcome, nor can I force a Spirit person to communicate. At times, it works better than others. I can't make the experience happen consciously. I have to feel the presence of Spirit blending with me; to be able to pass on the departed soul's thoughts. This happens naturally as I enter into a state of awareness and share my perceptions.

Mediumship is a passive experience. I need to remain open in my mind and allow the Spirit world to work with me. They manifest their information in whatever way it needs to come through me. I can't take control of that experience. It flows through me effortlessly – in my feelings, seeing, hearing, taste or smell; through my Spiritual senses.

When I am in the flow of communication, I have knowledge of information that is not normally available to me when I'm carrying out ordinary everyday tasks – for example, doing the dishes, sorting the laundry, hoovering, and so on. However, when I'm working and I'm tuning in to the mystical experience, I have access to a Spirit person. I can see their memories, character, personality, how they passed, names, hobbies, interests, family life and their work. The intelligence of the Spirit world means that they can communicate through my soul.

Mediumship is spontaneous. The experience doesn't last long. At a demonstration of mediumship, holding the power of communication with loved ones passed usually lasts only a few hours. I am unable to sustain the power after a certain amount of time. The power gradually wanes and tires, making the connection more difficult. I can't force information of a Spirit person to come. The flow of evidence moves through me. This flow is sustained by the power of God. When I feel the power dip, I know the contact is coming to a close.

Mediumship can transform lives. It has a positive impact on the sitter and on myself, transforming both of us. It can turn sceptics into believers. It can profoundly impact the individual whom I am working with.

Mystical experiences can't be repeated. Once it's manifested, it's gone forever. If I work with the same person, it will be different each time.

That's why I believe in the Miracle of Mediumship. It's a transient experience. Through awareness, I have knowledge of information I wouldn't normally be privy to. It happens without my control; as long as I engage in the experience and surrender to what I see, hear and feel. Mediumship has the power to change lives. It's used in service; to uplift, heal and bring positivity to another.

In the stories throughout this book and those in the following pages, I have worked with individuals who came to see me for a private consultation or demonstration. These are true, validated accounts from people who have experienced grief and loss. Because their loved ones from Spirit made connection with them, the Miracle of Mediumship has transformed their perspective and belief.

That is what mediumship is used for; to renew faith and provide hope. It is a reminder that your loved ones in Spirit are safe, well and happy. They continue to be present in your life, even when you can't sense them. I hope you gain comfort from reading these uplifting anecdotes.

CHAPTER FIFTEEN

Daddy Gerard

GERALDINE'S DAD WAS generally a fit man, rarely showing signs of illness. However, the family noticed he was starting to lose weight and seemed unable to stomach large meals. Over the years he would get check-ups, but doctors could never find anything.

When the family noticed that he was starting to look jaundiced, they urged him to see a doctor. His GP referred him to hospital immediately, where it was decided to keep him in for tests.

Despite staying in hospital, Gerard retained his sense of humour. "Did you pay much for this hotel?" he'd joke with his family. "Not much privacy here. Any chance of a wee brandy?"

Gerard was in hospital for ten days when the blood tests were returned. Doctors discovered he had multiple cancerous tumours. They had spread throughout his major organs; lungs, stomach, bowel and liver.

He was going to die.

The family were devasted. This wasn't the news they were expecting. Their dad had never given them any indication of pain. Sure, he sometimes had ailments, but nothing to merit a disease of this size.

The family asked if they could take Gerard home. They wanted to have some privacy with him; a chance for him to rest in the comfort of his own home. Unfortunately, the hospital wouldn't allow this, so he had to stay in the ward.

The family then asked if they could at least get him out of bed. His circulation wasn't good so they thought it would be nice to take him for a walk around the hospital. However, the nursing staff refused on the grounds of insurance. Added to that, they just didn't have the time.

After ten days of being in hospital, and only one day after his prognosis, Gerard suddenly took a blood clot and died.

Geraldine knew there were difficult days ahead and encouraged her mum to get some sleep. Overwhelmed with emotion herself, Geraldine went upstairs to get her mum's bed ready.

It was dark outside so Geraldine flicked on the

bedroom light and made her way over to draw the curtains. Just as she was approaching the glass pane, her dad's reflection appeared in the window. He was standing behind her. His appearance was exactly as she had seen a few hours earlier. Taking in the experience, she heard her dad's voice clearly in her mind.

"What happened to me?" he asked.

"You've died, daddy," she responded telepathically.

"Oh dear," she heard him say.

Geraldine turned to look at her dad, but he was gone.

Geraldine told her sister Toni about the experience. It comforted Toni and the family at the time. However, as the years went on, Toni kept thinking about her dad and wondering if he was okay. Toni had been seeing patterns of numbers since her dad passed and wondered if there was any reason behind it. She arranged to have a reading with me.

It was during the pandemic and I was taking video calls. The booking had been arranged through Toni's daughter, Maryann. When I arrived online, I saw both of them smiling at me. I explained briefly how I work, but I became aware immediately of Toni's dad standing to my left side.

"Toni, has your dad passed?" I enquired.

"Yes," she replied quickly.

"I feel your father is an extremely intelligent man," I began. "He is giving me the impression that he loved mathematics; solving problems. He's showing me that he travelled a lot with work. I feel he was some sort of engineer."

"Yes, dad was a nuclear engineer. He loved his job," she confirmed.

"He's talking about going to Scotland and England with work. He's also bringing me to South Africa. I feel he helped community projects while he was there. I'm seeing small villages and towns he helped. I'm not sure what the object of the desalination work was. He's showing me large concrete tunnels, mathematical drawings; plans." I relayed all of this to her, trying to explain the visions I was experiencing.

Toni nodded in agreement, confirming my statements. "Yes, our dad went to Africa! He worked on a desalination plant. They turn sea water into running water. He helped communities by providing fresh running water. This all makes sense to me!"

"I feel that your dad found it hard to switch off," I observed. "Even when he was at home, I can see him in the study. He's sitting at a brown wooden table; working on plans, organising. He loved keeping busy. I feel he was an incredibly attentive father, although I do feel that work was his primary purpose. He really leaned on your mum to keep the household going."

"Yes," Toni agreed. "Dad had a very scientific mind. He was devoted to his work; brilliantly academic, but he was still an extremely loving father. Mum and him were devoted parents. She took on the caring role while dad went to work and earned the money."

"Your dad's talking about the archaeologist in the family," I continued, expressing the visions and feelings that Toni's dad was relaying to me. "He seems interested in your work."

"Yes! That's my job!" Toni piped up, surprised. "I work as a forensic archaeologist. I help to find the missing dead."

"Wow, what an interesting job," I observed.

"Yes, I get to work all over Ireland; discovering and identifying graves. I've worked on some famous cases," she announced.

"I feel your dad is so proud of you; for all

your accomplishments, what you have achieved. He is making me feel like he was always encouraging your education when you were younger."

"Yes, that's right," Toni agreed. "Dad never made any difference between the sexes. He thought we should all have equal opportunities. He encouraged us to achieve our goals."

"He is prompting you to write a book about your work," I observed. "I feel people would find your experiences very interesting."

Toni raised her eyebrows in surprise. "I've been thinking about writing a book!"

"Maryann," I said, turning to Toni's daughter. "I know most of this reading is for your mum, but your grandad has a few words for you too. He's saying that you're going to be starting university soon. I keep seeing England, particularly near London. I feel your grandad is indicating that you will move across the water to study. He is giving me the feeling of you teaching."

Maryann laughed, "I've applied for Oxford University! It's close to London!"

"Remember your grandad's words," I told her. "Oh, and he's also telling me that you want a new car."

Toni laughed, "My husband and I were planning to buy a car for Maryann, but it was supposed to be a surprise!"

Joining in the laughter, I joked, "Well, I am only the messenger. You can blame your dad for spoiling the surprise!"

She waved her hand away light-heartedly, showing that she didn't mind. She was simply glad that the reading was going so well.

"He keeps giving me the name Gerard?" I threw out.

"Yes! That's dad name!" Toni confirmed, delighted.

"Well, please know that your dad loves you all very much. He wishes to pass on his love to your mother. His message to her is: when the time comes for her to join him, he will be waiting. They had a wonderful, long-lasting marriage," I could feel the love Gerard had for his wife and family.

"I hope you enjoyed the reading and got something from it," I said in closing, bringing the reading to an end.

"Oh, we loved it!" Toni exclaimed. "For a short period of time, Dad was back with us. Thank you so much."

Maryann got in touch with me a few months

after the reading. She let me know she had got a place in Oxford University. Maryann has since deferred Oxford to next year and has signed with an agent.

Gerard knew his grand-daughter would do well!

CHAPTER SIXTEEN

Daddy's Girl

2 FEBRUARY 2003 – a day that Ciara would never forget. Her dad died unexpectantly.

Ciara was incredibly close to her daddy, as was her sister and brother. Kevin, their dad, was a plumber by trade and taught apprentices in a local college.

Four years on, Ciara was sitting in an audience in front of me. Next to her, was mum Christine. It was New year and her dad's anniversary was fast approaching. It was also my first demonstration after the Christmas break and the room was packed with hopeful attendees.

Ciara and Christine really struggled with the loss of Kevin. A devoted husband and father, he had been the anchor for the family. It felt like their world had fallen apart.

However, like many families, they tried to just get on with everyday life. Ciara focused on her partner, their two young children and her hairdressing job.

I recognised the family. They used to be my sister's neighbours but they had moved away years ago. I also knew the circumstances of Kevin's death, although I hadn't seen or spoken to Ciara in a couple of years.

I normally prefer to work with strangers. However, if Spirit wants to pass a message on to someone I know, I will do it.

Addressing the audience, I informed them: "I don't normally work with people I know, but I do need to pass on this message."

Looking over at Ciara and Christine, I went on: "Kevin is here and I have to share his communication."

I set aside any scepticism people might have. Instead, I completely trusted that Spirit would give me evidence I couldn't possibly know. This would prove to Ciara and Christine that Kevin's soul still existed with them. That's exactly what happened.

I could feel Kevin's presence beside me, his thoughts were blending with mine, willing me to validate his existence to them.

Even though I was a little nervous, I allowed the information to flow.

"Ciara, can I come to you first? Your daddy is talking about your pregnancy."

Laughing, she called out: "Definitely not Angela! I already have two; no more for me!"

Everyone giggled at her response.

That didn't stop her dad. He wanted to pass on more information about this future vision.

"Well, he's showing me an image of you at a concert in Dublin. You're heavily pregnant in this vision. He's talking about another son."

Ciara was obviously doubtful. She wasn't pregnant and had no plans to expand the family, but Kevin was persistent.

"This is a little odd, but he's showing me an image of you building baby furniture on your own. He's almost puffing his chest out with pride. He's saying, *See? You're like me! You can use tools and build things*! He's talking about you building a set of drawers and a wardrobe for your new baby son."

Laughing and shaking her head in disbelief, Ciara affirmed, "No way Angela, I'm definitely not having any more kids."

Although laughing at her reaction, yet more information was streaming into my mind.

"I can see you getting engaged. It will be a

long engagement. Your dad is showing me that you'll get married in a chapel abroad."

"Right... okay," Ciara trailed off doubtfully. "I would like to get married abroad, but preferably on a beach."

Up until this point, Ciara couldn't relate to anything her daddy was sharing. How could she? It wasn't relevant to her life at that moment.

Turning to Christine, I felt that Kevin's love was now focused on her. "Kevin is saying he's so sorry about what happened. I know he was a brilliant family man. He's saying you are both soul mates. He still loves you, just as much as he did in life."

Christine's eyes glistened with tears, moved by his words.

"He's a funny guy, isn't he?" I smiled, allowing his humour to shine through. "He really loved himself; loved getting a tan, wearing nice clothes, doing his hair. I think he took longer getting ready than you did!"

Laughing, Christine agreed. "He took great pride in his appearance alright!"

"He knows you're planning to move house and he thinks it's a good idea. He's also talking about your son Conor. You're worrying about him, but Kevin is watching over him – please don't worry. He's going to do really well at university and he'll go on to have a successful career."

Continuing with Kevin's impressions on my mind, I told them: "Look for signs he gives you. He flicks the lights on and off to show you he's there."

"Yes! That's true! Our garage light keeps going on and off!" Christine exclaimed.

"Please know he loves you and will be with you whenever you need him."

Some time had passed and I hadn't seen Ciara or spoken to her. Out of the blue, she got in touch, excited to tell me her news.

"Angela, I just had to get in touch. I have to tell you what happened after you brought my daddy through that night," Ciara began. "I had no intention of getting pregnant again, but when I came back from my summer holiday, I found out I was expecting. I was shocked, but delighted!"

"You mentioned that you could see me at a concert in Dublin, heavily pregnant. I bought tickets to see Ed Sheeran in Croke Park, but I wasn't pregnant when I bought them. The following year when we went along, I was seven months pregnant!"

"You told me I'd be building baby furniture on my own. This also turned out to be true! I was supposed to build a set of drawers and wardrobe with my partner, but he got called in to work. I assembled them myself, just like daddy said I would!"

"You said I would have a boy. I really wasn't sure if you'd got this right. My partner and I paid a clinic to find out the sex of the baby. When we went along, the lady told us I was carrying a girl. I kept thinking back on the reading and what daddy said. He said that I'd have a boy, so I got another scan just to make sure. We actually ended up getting four scans in total! Every single one of them came back with same result: a girl. Obviously, we trusted the doctors and medical staff."

"Before the baby's birth, I bought everything in pink. I even picked a girl's name: Clodagh. At the baby shower, all the decorations were pink. Gifts from family and friends were all in pink: clothes, blankets, everything. I was convinced I was having a girl. With four scans confirming it, I thought you'd got that bit wrong."

"Before I went into hospital for the birth, I packed my case with all the pink baby grows and clothes. I was in labour for thirty-six hours and became extremely unwell. The doctors were very worried about me and the baby. I remember feeling that my daddy was there, holding my hand. I just knew he was there comforting me."

"The doctors made the decision to knock me out and give me an emergency section. Afterwards, I was groggy with medication and I didn't get to see or hold my baby initially. Everyone else knew what I had before I did. When I came around from the medication, I was shocked to be told I had given birth to a BOY. My daddy was completely right! All the scans had been incorrect."

She was laughing, recounting the story to me. "It was crazy, I couldn't believe it! I was so shocked. The whole thing just made me realise that he really must be with me. It gives me so much comfort and reassurance, knowing that he's always there."

"You mentioned that mummy would move house, which she did. My brother went on to achieve a first-class honours degree and he works for an amazing company. Me and mum couldn't relate to anything daddy was telling us that night, but everything worked out exactly as he said."

"My partner, Crawf, asked me to marry him four years ago. You said we would have a long engagement! We've planned to have our wedding in a church in Belamendia, Spain; not on a beach as I thought. Everything you said that night was completely spot on."

Nothing was relatable at the time; to me or to the family. Kevin knew about Ciara's life and the direction it would go in. He wanted to give her comfort that life would work out. He needed to share that kind of evidence that night. It may have taken a couple of years for everything to fall into place, but it finally gave them reassurance of his presence.

CHAPTER SEVENTEEN

Beautiful Caoimhe

I FIRST MET Noreen back in 2014 when she came to see me for a private reading. During that reading, I was able to see that her daughter Caoimhe was expecting Noreen's first grandchild. The family were naturally excited about the new arrival.

"I can see your daughter is having a son," I observed.

"Yes, that's correct," Noreen confirmed that they had found out the sex of the baby.

"I feel she'll be taken in on a Tuesday to have her labour induced, but she'll give birth on the Wednesday." I shared this information, trusting as always what I was experiencing.

Neither of us were sure of course if this would happen. Noreen recalls the reading as being positive and overall, she felt happy with it.

The next time I met Noreen she looked broken. It was as though the light within her had vanished. I knew she was grief-stricken however I didn't know at this point, that her daughter Caoimhe had died.

Caoimhe had passed 27 February 2016, two years after I had last read for Noreen.

Before we began, Noreen told me that after the last reading, her daughter did, in fact, give birth on a Wednesday. She had her son Jaden and then she got pregnant again shortly after and had her daughter Maddison.

I chuckled, saying that she must have her hands full. I didn't understand of course just how full Noreen's hands were, until we began the reading.

Closing my eyes, as I always do, I settled my thoughts and concentrated on the experience; what I was feeling, seeing and hearing. I asked God to give Noreen want she needed from the experience.

First, I was aware of Noreen's emotions; her mind, her thoughts and her feelings. I could feel that she was battling guilt, remorse and sadness. I knew she was feeling lost in life. I knew she was having to gather every ounce of strength to get through an intensely difficult time.

"Noreen, I know you're going through so much at the moment. I can feel that life is extremely difficult, both mentally and emotionally. Your head is all over the place."

As I was sharing, I could feel a young woman in Spirit. I knew it was her daughter.

"I have a young female here. She's a young adult, only around twenty-one."

"Yes, my daughter was twenty-one when she died," Noreen whispered.

"I feel you looked similar, almost like sisters. You were so alike in personality, even in your mannerisms; your attitude to life. You were always so close."

"I have to be honest here, Noreen, did she kill herself?" I asked, softly, even though I already knew the answer from Spirit.

Noreen heaved a sigh of sorrow and emotion: "Yes."

"Immediately I can feel her regret. She's apologising to you and the family."

"I will come back to her passing in a moment, but first I want to talk about her personality," I began. "She's so outgoing; a fun-loving, bubbly, huge personality. She was very jokey and loved making people laugh, didn't she?"

"Yes," Noreen wiped a tear away, half-chuckling, half-crying. "She was the life and soul of our house."

"She's giving me the name Caoimhe," I announced.

"Yes, that's right!" Noreen confirmed, surprised.

"I feel she was a real drama queen," I observed bravely, feeling Caoimhe's rebellious soul. "She wasn't afraid to defend herself; to speak out if need be. I actually think she could be quite cheeky at times!"

Laughing, Noreen agreed.

"She's talking about hating school. She loved her friends and the fun she had with her mates, but she hated studying. Maths, Science and Religion were a complete bore to her, although she loved drama. It suited her outgoing personality. She's talking about her love for dance and singing. She's making me aware that dancing was a huge part of her life. I'm getting memories of her being involved in a dance group. It made her feel alive. She's talking about singing everywhere she went." I let the flow of information stream out.

'Yes, Caoimhe was in a hip-pop group called Rapture. She'd been in it since she was seven years old. She loved singing and dancing. My younger daughters followed in her footsteps. She always entertained us and had us laughing!"

"I can see her in my mind," I said, using my hand to mimic primping myself. "She's laughing; saying to me: 'Look, I'm gorgeous!' She's slim, tanned, wears lovely clothes. She had great style. Always looked after her hair and nails. She enjoyed pampering herself."

"Yes!" Noreen chuckled affectionately. "Everyone used to comment on her clothes; asking her where she'd bought them. She had a great eye for fashion. She loved herself!"

"I feel she was loud; she argued with people, especially her boyfriend. She could always stand up for herself, to anyone – man or woman. You brought her up to defend her beliefs."

Smiling at the memories of her daughter, Noreen recalled a story about Caoimhe. Her brother had been arguing with another guy and Caoimhe stepped in to stick up for him.

"She was very protective of her siblings," Noreen nodded, her chest puffed with pride.

"She's talking about the night she died," I said, my tone becoming more serious. "She argued with her boyfriend. She had bought him a new tracksuit, but then she saw his sister wearing it. It kickstarted a disagreement between all of them."

"I'm not sure," Noreen admitted. "No-one ever told me what actually happened that night. Caoimhe lived with me but she was staying with her boyfriend at the time. I was having the house redecorated; a new bathroom and kitchen fitted, re-wiring. The house was upside down. I knew she had bought him a new tracksuit; I didn't realise there was an argument over it."

"She's taking me back to the night she died," I said, fanning my fingers out and seeing the image in my mind's eye. "I can see a graveyard. It's in the Whiterock area. She's bringing me up to a tree beside a wall in the cemetery. She's saying these are her last memories; she died in the cemetery." I looked at Noreen with sadness. "I feel she didn't truly mean it. It was an accident. She's saying that when she looks back, she knows she had an amazing life."

Tears poured from Noreen's face as her shoulders heaved with emotion. "Yes, I think it was just a moment of madness," she sobbed. "I'm the one who found her."

Noreen wiped her tears away with a tissue, but more kept falling. "I had got a phone call from her boyfriend's family that day. They told me she'd gone missing. It wasn't like her. She was the type of person who didn't even like going to the shop on her own."

"We all went looking for her," Noreen went on, recalling that awful day. "Something inside me told me to look in the graveyard. When I went there, I looked up at the tree and saw her suspended." Noreen's voice choked with tears.

"We rang for an ambulance straight away, but deep in my heart, I knew it was too late. The paramedic who worked on her said he'd never seen anyone so beautiful. He wasn't able to save her unfortunately."

Noreen heaved a sigh, her heart heavy. "I know it was a moment of madness. There's no way she would leave her two kids."

We were both crying by now. I was just as emotional as Noreen. My heart was broken for this amazing, courageous mother who had gone through such a tragic and traumatic event.

"She really loves you," I shared. "She loves her children and her siblings. She doesn't want anyone blaming themselves."

"She's saying, *'I don't blame you mum for my passing. I don't blame my boyfriend. It wasn't anyone fault.'*"

I went on, relaying Caoimhe's earnest message: "She really struggled with her mental
health. Life was like an emotional roller-coaster.
One day she'd be high as a kite; full of life; happy,
planning loads. The next day, she'd be down in
the dumps, unable to do anything. Her head was
all over the place; it was hard to get any balance."

"She's talking about her children now," I went
on. "She's happy that you got to be legal guardian
of her kids. I feel it's been a real struggle with the
courts and the legal system but you got there."

"Yes, I'm sole carer of the kids. Jaden was two
years old when it happened and Maddison was
only one. I've been taking care of them alongside
my other children."

"I feel your grand-daughter will be very like
her mum; the cheekiness, her mannerisms and
attitude. Your grandson will be different; more
reserved, quiet, deeper."

Noreen nodded in agreement.

"She loved her children very much and still
does," I stated.

Caoimhe was showing me visions ahead from
Spirit. She expressed her concerns for her children.

"She's saying that for all they've gone

through, they're coping okay. They're supported and loved. They'll do well at school."

"She's adding jokingly '*Unlike me!*'"

Noreen chuckled at her daughter's confession.

"I know that your mother passed away some time ago too, Noreen," I said softly.

Noreen nodded sadly.

"I can feel that your daughter is with your mum now. They are together in Spirit."

Noreen smiled, comforted by this news.

Information from Caoimhe kept streaming into my thoughts. "Caoimhe's joking now and saying that she always got her way with you. I think she had you wrapped around her wee finger!"

Noreen laughed gently, acknowledging this truth.

"She was always borrowing money from you. You would give her grief about it," I teased. "But she knew fine well she'd never have to pay you back!"

Bringing the reading to a close, I passed on Caoimhe's final words: "She wants to remind you how much she loves you and she wants you to know she's doing well. I feel she helps lots of young people in Spirit. She also helps young people on this side of life; especially with mental health and thinking patterns. She still has work to do, but she's staying positive. She'll never lose that big personality. Nor will she ever lose her love for you and the family."

Caoimhe was, and continues to be, a beautiful soul. Her light radiated wherever she went. Joy, love and humour emanated from her.

She is now safe in the loving arms of the angels and her grandmother. Caoimhe has found peace in Spirit. Like all souls who pass in this tragic way, no one is lost. Consciousness lives on. Spirit wants to prove their existence to those who matter the most; to help those closest know they are secure and well.

Caoimhe passed away in a shocking and upsetting way. Her love for her mum, children and wider family was evident. She will never leave their side. Individuals who do take their own life are embraced with the same love and acceptance as every person is. There is no place of limbo, suffering or purgatory. No one is judged. The Spirit world is home. It's a place of freedom and joy. Our souls feel no pain. Relatives greeted Caoimhe. Her granny was there to show her the way. She is protected. She talked about the work she does in Spirit to help young people with mental health. Caoimhe wants to be of service, improving people's perspective, reminding people that no one is alone.

The light of the Spirit encompasses all souls, God's love embraces each person continually.

CHAPTER EIGHTEEN

Natasha's Story

WHEN NATASHA GOT accepted for Winchester University in England, a new and exciting chapter in her life was about to unfold. With her creative talents and interest in dance, Natasha had ambitions of becoming a choreographer.

Natasha, a fun-loving girl with an outgoing personality, easily attracted friends. Settling into the campus, she acquainted herself with everyone, but it was one lad who caught her eye. Pat was not only easy-going; he was easy on the eye!

Pat was studying Media and Film studies and coincidentally, his bedroom was next door to hers. Always making her laugh, his charming and cheeky charisma won Natasha over. They formed an instant bond and were inseparable friends.

Natasha cared deeply for Pat. She would get upset if girlfriends dumped him. Likewise, Pat would get angry at other lads for mistreating her. It was clear to both of them that they had deeper feelings for each other.

It wasn't until after university that they allowed themselves to take their friendship to the next level. It was the right time. They were happy to have waited as a romantic relationship would have been too much pressure during their studies.

As their bond deepened, it felt natural to plan towards the future. They set up home together, finding a flat. They talked of marriage and having children. Both of them felt their future together was fate; synchronicity of meeting at university. Natasha and Pat knew they were soul mates. They adored each other and her heart firmly belonged to his.

It was nearing Christmas time and Pat had arranged to meet up with two friends for drinks. Natasha didn't like Pat associating with these friends as she felt they were a negative influence. Pat's drinking could be heavy at times.

Her anxiety was different this night. She felt sick in her stomach and argued with him, pleading with him to stay at home. Pat reasoned that he'd be alright and reassured her that he'd be home soon.

Pat left their home for Maidstown to see his

friends. This was on 13th December 2014. Natasha's stomach churned as he closed the green door of their flat.

Unsettled, she waited up all night for his return. Something wasn't right, she just knew it. Pacing the floors, she rang his mobile a few times but he didn't answer. He would normally ring her on a night out; this was so out of character. Not ringing back; not picking up his phone; not arriving home at a decent hour. *Where is he?*

Tossing and turning, Natasha eventually fell asleep. When she woke again at around 4am, there was still no sign of Pat. Her apprehension was strangely settled with a feeling of peace and she dozed off for a few more hours.

Waking the following morning, she checked immediately for Pat. Still nothing.

Feeling frustrated and irritated, she tried to get ready for work.

Where is he? Why hasn't he come home?

In work, Natasha kept ringing Pat over and over. Still nothing.

Checking her phone later, she noticed several missed calls from one of the mates he'd been out with. Panic set in. She just *knew* something had happened. Natasha didn't like this guy to start with, but perhaps someone could shed some light on what was going on. The friend was just as concerned as Natasha, telling her that Pat had gone missing on the night out. Pat was pretty drunk and the lads assumed he had gone home.

This is so unlike him, she thought, fear enveloping her. *No-one has seen him.*

Alarmed by the call, Natasha left work in a panic. Ringing around as many people she could think of, she asked if anyone had heard from Pat. No-one knew; none of his family or friends.

Asking her friends to help find Pat, she tried not to let her fear overwhelm her.

He'll be back soon, she told herself optimistically. *This isn't my Pat, I'll find him.*

Another day passed with no news.

Dread loomed over Natasha as she decided it was time to report it to the Police. Filing a missing person's report for Pat felt surreal and terrifying. *Was this really happening?*

There wasn't an ounce of peace for Natasha; her mind was riddled with anxiety. Every waking moment of the day, she prayed that her beautiful soulmate would walk in through the door. The love of her life.

Refusing to give up hope, Natasha searched

the town high and low; all the bars, shops and streets. She knocked on doors, asking if anyone had seen him. She even tried drug dens in case he had somehow ended up there.

Please God, Angels, Saints; please bring him home to me.

The days crawled along. Local media began reporting Pat's case. Not only were friends and family searching, but kind strangers had joined in. Search and rescue teams were inspecting river banks. Police checked CCTV and spotted Pat on the night he went missing. He was last seen in a pub called 'House of Home'.

The footage showed him stumbling out of the bar, going next door to get food and then returning to the pub. Police discovered that he had been kicked out of the bar for being too drunk.

The CCTV showed the last time Pat was sighted. He was staggering across the main road adjacent to the river Medway, Kent.

Natasha spent every moment of every day searching for her best friend and devoted partner. She sent out appeals online and in the local neighbourhood. No stone was left unturned. She just wanted him safely back in her arms.

On the twenty-eighth day of Pat's disappearance, Natasha received the worst possible news. Pat's remains had been discovered.

Heaving, the horror of the news set in. Natasha's world crashed. Inconsolable, her heart felt like it had been ripped out of her chest. *How could this have happened? Why?*

Desperate to find answers, Natasha phoned the Police constantly, asking for updates.

Over the coming weeks, the police were able to piece together his last movements. He had walked along the river banks, accidently fell into the water and drowned.

A local resident found Pat in the marina of the River Medway. He was ten miles downstream from the pub he had been drinking in. It took almost a month to locate his body.

Pat was only twenty-eight years old.

The devastation of Pat's passing plummeted Natasha into a spiral of depression and suicidal thoughts. Her future plans were shattered and it felt like her life was over. She was desperate to know if he was somehow still with her, even after death. She needed to know if he was okay and it became her primary focus.

A friend suggested a local group called 'Footsteps' that held weekly evenings of mediumship.

Mediums from around the country were asked to attend. Any money raised was donated towards the special care baby unit.

It was at that point that I received an invite from Footsteps to attend. Feeling both excited and nervous, it was my first time working in England. My friend Andy, who was also a guest medium, drove us to the event.

The organiser Julie greeted us both with a big smile. Leading us into a quiet room, she gave us space to prepare ourselves. I sat in silence, closing my eyes, praying and connecting with a spiritual power.

"God, give these people whatever you feel will help them."

I have learned over the years to surrender to God's will; to trust the subtle feelings and visions that come into my mind and body. Feeling mentally prepared, we set off into the hall to link with loved ones in Spirit.

Julie welcomed everyone in the audience and introduced Andy and me as the guest mediums. I glanced around and smiled at everyone, but I was also beginning to *tune in*; to feel where Spirit wanted me to work in the room.

I noticed a young girl sitting in the front row,

next to a slightly older lady. They reassembled one another and I guessed it was mum and daughter. The daughter was smiling over at me. I hadn't met either of them before, but I was beginning to feel and see in my mind's eye a young man standing with her in Spirit. I knew he was keen to let her know he was okay.

As Andy finished his demonstration, it was my turn to work. I went straight over to her and began: "I feel I have a young lad here in Spirit. He's stood next to you. I feel he accidentally drowned. Does that make sense to you?"

"Yes!" Natasha replied excitedly.

I could feel the urgency of this young man's soul. "He's making me aware that his body wasn't found immediately. It was a missing person's case initially. I can see helicopters. Hundreds of people from the local community came out to help search for him."

Filling up with tears, she nodded her head, showing that it was resonating with her. Her mum reached out to hold her hand.

"The police didn't do much in your eyes, you were angry with them," I continued.

Shocked but delighted, Natasha explained, "Yes, it took twenty-eight days to find him. We were going to go to the Head of Police to complain."

"I feel someone else found him, not the Police. He feels sorry for the person who found him. I feel it haunts them."

Natasha agreed that this was accurate.

More details kept coming to me about his passing. "He remembers that you both argued before he left that night. I feel he was drinking before he passed. He's saying that he was drunk and bumped his head; that it was an accident."

Natasha agreed that he had been out with two friends.

"He feels like a boyfriend," I said.

"Yes, we knew each other for about ten years. He was my partner," Natasha shared wistfully.

Feeling her anguish and despair, I wanted to keep going. I could feel him very close to her. "Your partner is showing me clairvoyantly, a vision of an amusement park where he won you a huge monkey with a banana." I laughed at the image.

"Frank!" Natasha's mum called out.

Confused, I looked over at her mum.

"We named the monkey *Frank*," her mum explained. "We kept him in the living room because he was too big for the bedroom." A ripple of laughter rang out among the audience.

Smiling, I continued: "I feel you both met in University."

"Yes, that's correct. We met and studied in Uni together," Natasha confirmed.

"I really feel you were both soul mates. He loves you deeply. He wants you to know he is safe. He's sorry for breaking your heart," I shared softly. I could feel he was trying so hard to let her know he was still deeply in love with her.

"He talks about you wearing his clothes in bed at night," I told her.

Natasha nodded emotionally. "I got his clothes made into a patchwork quilt. I wrap it around me every night."

"He's saying you've done some DIY for him today," I mentioned, light-heartedly.

Natasha smiled, informing us all that she had put up some photographs of him in her bathroom that morning.

The information kept flowing to me to about his beautiful partner.

"He sees you writing love letters to him. He loves this. He also wants to thank your mum for all the support and love she has given you."

Both Natasha and her mother started to cry.

"He is a strong communicator. I know he will continue to love and support you," I shared, the connection with Pat now starting to fade.

"Everyone needs to remember that love is the most important thing," Natasha announced.

"I couldn't agree more," I replied.

At the end of the evening, Natasha and her mum came up to me and introduced themselves. They told me what happened that tragic night with Pat.

Natasha took great comfort from the realisation that Pat was still present in her life. The details that Pat relayed, such as the monkey, were surprising yet accurate. My wish for Natasha was to be reassured of Pat's continuing love to her. She need never feel alone; he will always be around.

Natasha described the reading as: *"Something has lifted from my heart and I feel more at peace."*

CHAPTER NINETEEN

Connie, The Dancing Queen

CONNIE ADORED HER partner and family, but her biggest passion in life was dancing. A hard-working and independent girl, she loved to let her hair down with a Saturday night boogie. No alcohol was needed when Connie hit the dance floor. She'd be up, showing off her dance moves.

As a teenager, Connie couldn't afford dance lessons, but that didn't stop her ambition. Money was tight in the family home so Connie learned to make her own costumes. Finding spare bits of material, she'd sew them together to create flashy outfits.

Dancing was Connie's creative outlet; her channel of expression. She even went on to win Miss UK Champion, gaining the reputation of being one of the best disco dancers of her time. Her medals and trophies were displayed with pride of place on the mantelpiece.

At one point, Connie wanted to work as a

choreographer, but instead she decided to help adolescents in the local youth centre. Giving up her spare time, she taught dancing free of charge. She wanted to encourage youngsters not only to gain body image confidence, but just to have fun!

Connie wouldn't have considered herself to be good-looking, but with her long, curly brown hair and stunning figure, one would have argued otherwise.

It was her bubbly personality that was truly intoxicating though. She loved to laugh and brought a smile to everyone's lips. People felt uplifted when Connie was around. Because she loved helping people, her empathy and compassion drew her into the health care profession. Training in the ambulance service and planning to marry her partner Brian, life was going well for Connie. Happy and content, they had a desire to start a family of their own.

Connie was only twenty-four when she was diagnosed with Non-Hodgkin's Lymphoma, a type of cancer that develops in the lymphatic system.

With her medical background, Connie knew the difficulties that lay ahead. Thanks to a loving partner and family, she began to lean on them for support. For the next three years, she didn't give up hope.

Connie had an extra special bond with her sister. Nichola the eldest, was the protective one, always keeping an eye on Connie, the youngest. Growing up, their family home was so modest that Connie and Nichola shared a bed together. It was a tight squeeze at times but the two sisters enjoyed their childhood. They always had a laugh together and rarely had any disagreements.

Connie's cancer came as a terrible blow to Nichola and the family circle. Feeling powerless to help, the news only reinforced her love and concern for Connie.

Connie took the doctors' advice and tried all the recommended treatments. Her beautiful long curly hair fell out. It did grow back eventually, although the curls never returned.

Brian asked Connie to be his wife. When he proposed, she was still very unwell, but that didn't stop her joy. They planned the wedding, but brought it forward due to her declining health. On January 2003, she walked down the aisle. It was a magical day. The syringe driver strapped to her leg for pain relief didn't stop her enjoying the first dance. Thoughts of illness were replaced with dance and fun. She savoured very moment of the special day, cherishing her newly-wed husband and the loved ones around her.

Eight months later, Connie passed away.

On the day of the funeral, thousands of mourners paraded the streets. Ambulances and paramedic colleagues lined the roads in her honour. The neighbourhood came to a standstill. Everyone wanted to show their respects.

It was a terrible blow to Connie's sister and the family and it was the first time Nichola had ever experienced grief. It was only one week after the funeral when Nichola became aware of her sister's presence. Nichola could feel her; she knew Connie was standing beside her in Spirit. It was a real experience.

Nichola began finding white feathers in strange places. She could feel that her sister was trying to let her know she was there; that she wasn't alone.

Nichola's friend Claire bought tickets for their group of pals to come and see my work. By now, it was August 2021 – a whole eighteen years since Connie had passed. My event also happened to be the same week as Connie's anniversary.

As I stood on the stage, I looked out to a room

full of hopeful people; each one of them eagerly awaiting messages from loved ones. As always, I had that nervous feeling in the pit of my stomach. My work is never scripted and I never know what's going to happen. I have to trust completely in Spirit; to be open to the contact I am about to experience.

Closing my eyes, I became conscious of the Spirit people around me. They began to lead me to parts of the room where their loved ones were sitting. Opening my eyes again, I started to relay the information I was being given. The flow of information was very strong and I could feel them close; eager to share their love and words of encouragement to family and friends.

I became aware of a sister with me in Spirit. I knew her sibling was present and she needed to get a message to her. My energy was being pulled to a specific part of the room.

"Can I come to you please?" I enquired, going directly to a lady wearing a blue top. She had short brown hair and looked mid-forties or early fifties.

"Who me?" she asked, surprised.

"Yes, I have a sister here with me. I know she was very sick before she passed. I feel it was cancer. Does that make sense?"

"Yes," Nichola gulped, her eyes widened.

"It was such a shock when she was diagnosed. Prior to that, she was very fit and healthy. She knew she was dying and she was still very young when she passed; around twenty-nine," I said, relaying the information to Nichola.

"Yes, my sister was twenty-seven when she passed away," Nichola clutched her hand to her mouth, surprised by my revelation.

"She really loved dancing. It was her passion. I know most women love getting out for a wee dance," I said, waving my hand energetically. "But it was more than that. She's showing me that she taught dance to young ones. She wanted to help build their confidence. She entered a lot of dancing competitions – it was a huge part of her life. I feel your sister had thought about dancing as a career at one stage, but it wasn't her job."

Nichola was focused in on every word I was sharing; nodding in agreement to all my statements.

"Connie's soul was strong," I continued. "She's showing me that you've recently been looking through old photographs of her from her dancing days. She's dressed up in the photos. I can see newspaper clippings – they're all in a memory box. She knows you cried looking at the old pictures of her. She's saying to you, 'I haven't forgotten about you. You're still my sister. I love you no matter how long I'm passed. Me and you – we were inseparable.' "

Overwhelmed with emotion, Nichola clutched a tissue, dabbing it at the corner of her eyes.

"I know you were like best friends. You think to yourself at times, 'I wonder is she okay?' You get signs from her all the time – angel feathers in your path."

"Yes! I got one today!" Nichola exclaimed.

"Well, perhaps her turning up tonight is one of your biggest signs," I smiled.

"She's showing me someone close to you works as a care worker," I went on.

"Yes, that's my daughter," Nichola confirmed.

"Can I ask, is she expecting at the moment?"

Nichola threw her hands up to her mouth: "Oh my God, yes!"

"Your sister is saying, yes, I know she's pregnant and she's expecting a son."

Everyone in the audience gasped and looked towards Nichola to see her reaction.

"Yes! We found out she's having a boy!"

Nichola cried.

"She's saying: 'I'm watching your growing family. I see the positive things coming into your life. Congratulations! I may not be there in person but I'm celebrating here in Spirit. I'm with you on your journey.'"

"'Relax!' She's saying. 'Stop panicking about things. I'm doing a happy dance for you'." I jiggled my hips, mimicking Connie's dance from Spirit.

"Over the years, you weren't sure whether to believe it, but you experienced her voice in your mind. Always a loving voice. Know that it's your sister reaching out to you personally. She's so proud of you," I reassured Nichola.

"She keeps saying, 'I'm still dancing here! I couldn't enjoy dancing properly before I died. I had lost so much weight and was so sick, but I'm dancing now!'"

With her closing words of reassurance and comfort, Connie's contact began to fade softly.

The family came up to chat to me at the end of the evening. They told me about Connie's life and how it fitted in with everything she had shared during the reading.

"I was totally overwhelmed what came

through," Nichola gushed. "She danced all the time. And it's true, my daughter IS expecting. I already have five grandsons and now a sixth is due. When I get a granddaughter, Connie's name will be passed on to her."

Emotional, Nichola went on: "I'm so happy to know she's okay. She's always on my mind; my beautiful little sister."

Loved ones are keen to let us know they are still watching over us. They know the events that take place in our lives and want to comfort us.

Spirt are whole, light and free from illness. Letting go of all pain when they die, there is no sickness or disability. They are in a place of healthiness, vibrancy and wellness.

"Think of me as healthy. That's how I am in Spirit. When you look at my photos, that's how I look here. I'm energised!'"

CHAPTER TWENTY

John, My Brother

OPENING THE DOOR to Laura, I first notice her striking blue eyes. Ushering her in, we make our way up to my work room. As Laura sits facing me, I take in more of her appearance. Her face appears tired and distraught, as though she's carrying the weight of the world on her shoulders.

We exchange a few pleasantries before we settle in to the reading. She presses the record button on her mobile and I begin.

"I have your brother, John here."

Immediately, I could feel John's humorous personality. He wants to break the ice.

"He sure is self-confident about his looks," I laugh. "He thought he was God's gift to women."

Laura giggled. "Aye, that's right, all the women were besotted by him!"

Amused by John's character, I went on, "It was really important to him how he looked; how he dressed. He's saying, 'Look at my teeth! They're lovely and white!'"

Laura chuckled: "Yes, we were always telling John to get his teeth whitened. He had lovely teeth, but they were discoloured because he smoked so much."

"'I can hear him laughing. 'Well, they're white now!'" I grinned.

"He's saying, 'Thank you for putting my shoes on, along with my three-piece grey suit'. He loved how you dressed him in the coffin."

"That's exactly what we dressed him in!" Laura beamed.

"He's joking again – He's saying, 'Thanks very much for cutting the side of my hair – you left a big bald patch!" I began stroking the side of my head to show Laura where he was pointing to.

Laura clasped her hand to her mouth: "Yes! I cut a whack of his hair off when he was in the coffin – from that exact spot you're pointing to! I did it when everyone went to bed. I wanted to keep it for my mummy and sister."

I carried on relaying his messages: "He's delighted that you got the signet ring back from the coroner too."

Laura grinned: "Yes! His daughter Maeve

wears his ring around her neck on a gold chain now."

The information kept pouring in: "He also wants to thank you for the beautiful letter you wrote after he died. He knows you placed it secretly in the coffin."

Filling up with tears, Laura sobbed: "Yes, when John died, his coffin was returned to our family home. I was in such a bad place. To be honest, I didn't want to be here any longer. I wrote him a five-page letter sharing how I felt about him. I talked about our close relationship. No-one knew I placed that letter in the coffin, just me."

"I have to be honest here, Laura," I said softly. "I know there are more struggles to come, but he'll be with you, giving you all the strength you need."

"He's talking about solicitors now," I went on. "Legal papers, court."

John had always been a successful business man, but a legal issue arose which gave him a lot of stress. Being the independent and proud man that he was, he kept his worries to himself.

"There are legal battles ahead. It will get nasty."

I had to be honest with her. I really didn't want to worry her, especially since she had just only buried her brother. On the other hand, I felt it was important to relay everything John wanted to tell her.

John then changed the direction of the reading away from business issues. Instead, he showed me a tragic image of Laura. She was standing on a boardwalk, wanting to jump in.

"I know this isn't funny in the slightest Laura, but John is trying to joke about a really difficult subject. He's making an off-the-cuff comment about you wanting to jump into the water to be with him. He's laughing, saying he was going to throw you in with him, but then you'd have died from hypothermia."

Stunned, Laura couldn't help but smile at his dry humour. "Oh my God, he's such a buck eejit. That's so like our John with his quick wit."

"He's saying, 'Please stop thinking like that because mummy needs you. I also need you – I need you to be a role model for my daughter."

Laura admitted: "Before I came for this reading, I went for a walk along the Titanic boardwalk. I try to walk every day since John passed. It usually helps to clear my head. But today, when I was standing on the water's edge, I just kept thinking, 'I wish I had the courage to throw myself in. Then I could be with John'."

"I feel that John's way of dealing with things is to try to be funny, but he's concerned about you Laura. He's very protective over you and loves you very much."

"Yes, I know he does," Laura sighed. "But he can be a wee shit at times too!" Despite the sadness, we both laughed thinking of John's wit and sarcasm.

"He's giggling, saying, 'I'm walking around your apartment and you need your kitchen tap fixed. You'll also need a new fridge soon."

Laura rolled her eyes playfully: "Oh, he knew full well they needed fixed. He's a plumber and he never got round to fixing it before he passed. Tell him thanks very much!"

"He's with you at night when you can't sleep," I went on. "He hears you calling out his name, asking if he'd show himself to you."

I suppressed a smile as I continued: "He's laughing saying, 'If I showed myself to you, you'd die of a heart attack. You wouldn't cope!"

We both laughed, Laura agreeing this would be the case.

When Laura first walked in, she appeared tired and broken, but now she was laughing, recognising John's humour and joviality.

"He's telling me that his passing was sudden. When he died, your granny Mary and your daddy John came to meet him, embracing him on the other side. He's not on his own Laura," I reassured her.

"Your brother is saying, 'When I died, the ambulance got there really quickly, but I had already gone. He's showing me he died in his bed. Your dad and granny were there in Spirit waiting for him."

"I can feel them all together here with us, but today it's John's turn to speak. He's the one you need to hear from the most."

"He's laughing again, Laura. He's saying, 'You know, you can travel anywhere you want over here! For free!'"

Laura chuckled, remembering his love for travel. "Oh, he's still adventurous then?"

Laura's job involved travelling to Europe and America. John sometimes accompanied her, sharing their love of travel.

"He's saying, 'Keep an eye out for the bundle of money in my house when you're clearing it out.'"

Laura widened her eyes in surprise: "Oh, I definitely will!"

When they did a clear out of John's belongings, they found some notes in Dutch Kroner. It must have been left over from his travels to Copenhagen.

"He's so proud of the size of the funeral," I shared.

"Yes, hundreds of people lined the road for him. It was a huge funeral," Laura agreed.

Opening up emotionally, she shared her fond memories: "My brother was funny, witty, sarcastic. He partied hard, living life to the full. He loved us and he loved his daughter. He was generous to a fault. It was only after he died that we discovered he had been paying for a friend's mortgage. That's the kind of person he was; always putting others before himself."

"There's one more thing he's sharing," I said, feeling that his contact was coming to a close. "He's talking about your close family friend. Keep an eye on him. If there's any pain or discomfort in his chest, make sure he gets it seen to immediately. Watch out for any heart problems."

A week after the reading, a close friend of the family had a heart scare and was rushed to hospital.

Bringing the reading to a close, Laura shared her gratitude. Overwhelmed by how much information had come through, she said: "This has given me so much hope. It's such a comfort to know I'll see him again one day."

Before leaving, she told me: "You know, the weekend before he died, we chatted on the phone. He was about to head to his girlfriend's house in Scotland. My last words to him were: 'Life's too short. Go and enjoy yourself.'"

CHAPTER TWENTY-ONE

An Unbreakable Bond

"HI, I'M DIANE. I'm here to see Angela for my reading today."

"Yes, I'll just call her now and let her know you're here," my mum responded.

I was upstairs in my room sending thoughts to Spirit; to give my next client all that she needed from me. It's important to have some quiet time before a reading.

I heard my mum call from downstairs: "Angela, your next client is here."

With faith that Spirit would help, I walked down the two flights of stairs and greeted a small, slim lady with long dark hair. She was elegant in her style of clothes.

"Hi, Angela," Diane greeted me in her soft, gentle tone.

"Hi, Diane, come upstairs and we'll give it a go," I smiled. We climbed the stairs towards my work room. Making small talk, it gave us both a chance to relax for a few moments, before I began tuning into loved ones passed.

Sitting opposite one another, she was quiet (almost distant at first), when I tried to interact with her. I knew from her expression that she needed to connect to someone important from Spirit.

Admittedly, I was a little nervous. Sometimes it can be daunting. I'm well aware of people's expectations. Their needs, desires and hopes are all put upon my shoulders. Most people who come for a reading are hoping to connect with one or two people in Spirit. I have to trust that God will help me.

I went through my usual routine of explaining how I work, which seemed to settle us both. Diane pressed the record button on her mobile. I closed my eyes, moving my awareness inwardly. Tuning in to all I was experiencing, I began to notice any subtle changes. I listened for any visions, thoughts or words I had to express.

I became aware of Diane's grandparents first, describing them on point. Then a cousin of the family came through to connect. Again, there was a lovely flow of information. However, I knew that neither of those communicating were 'the one'.

"Hold on a moment," I said. "I can feel some-one else. There's a young man here and he's making me laugh. He wants to come in with this grand entrance," I laughed.

Diane began to relax slightly, showing a slight smile.

I knew he was 'the one'.

"What I notice about him straight away is that he's wearing a beanie hat," I observed. "I feel he loved hats. He's showing me his room where he had a collection of hats. He wore them every day." I began with the stream of images and feelings flowing into my mind.

"Yes, that's right, he loved hats," Diane con-firmed. "He always wore one."

"I feel he was a real mummy's boy. For a young man, he still very much showed his affection towards you," I said, feeling his gentle nature. "He remembers texting 'I love you' if he was heading out. He never thought it was soft."

"He loved fun and banter," I went on. "But his nature was more laid back. His personality had a very calming influence towards people." I shared feeling his soul's essence.

"He is trying to calm you," I told Diane. "He's saying; 'You're going to be alright. You will get through this.' He wants to help you with your anxiety. There are some areas of your life that are difficult to face at the moment. He knows it has been hard."

"Yes, yes it has," Diane agreed softly, her eyes welling up.

Changing the mood slightly, I admitted: "He's laughing now. Mischievous. He's telling me that he's been playing up with the electrics in your home. The lights have been flickering on and off, the television playing up. He's just been trying to get your attention."

"He was a good lad," I went on. "Never causing any bother. He remembers his role as the man of house. He sees himself as the protector towards you all. You could lean on him, ask him for advice and help. He was mature for his age. He remembers always wanting to give back to you. He wanted a bigger house; to pay off your mortgage, to help you where needed. He really loved you and wanted to take care of you. That's why he's so protective of you. This must be your son, Diane" I told her.

"Calvin, my son, did see himself as the man of the house. There was only me, him and his sister at the time," she responded emotionally. "He was always thinking about other people first."

"He's saying, 'Get out of the house more, mum. You're overthinking about everything'. He wants more fun for you. He wants your energy to feel uplifted. As I bring in the word 'fun', he's showing me an image of him playing the guitar. He wasn't a professional or in a band or anything," I laughed. "But I know he attempted making up his own songs, played around with it. It was a hobby of his, does that make sense?" I asked.

"Yes, yes," Diane smiled. She was quietly spoken, but agreed with all that Calvin was sharing.

"His skills were basic, but he definitely enjoyed playing his own rifts," I chuckled. "He loved bands like Oasis and that genre of music, slightly rocky. I don't feel he enjoyed dance music at all."

"Yes, that's all correct," Diane confirmed. "He loved rock music."

"He's showing me Bob Dillion, The Doors; he loved older rock groups too."

"Yes, he loved all of those artists," Diane agreed.

"He's bringing me now to your local pub. You

must live in a small town. I feel it's a place where everyone knows each other's business. He remembers it as a tight-knit community. I feel there were only a few bars in the town. He didn't drink too much, but he did enjoy the odd pint with his mates." I told her, feeling the flow of Calvin's memories.

"He disliked arguments or fights," I carried on. "He had a laid-back nature, but he does recall a night in the local pub when a friend got into a fight. Your son was always amicable. He tried to break up the fight, but he got caught in the brawl. He had a few marks on his face – nothing serious, but his nose and face were bleeding. This only happened once, do you remember?"

"Yes, I remember he came home and went straight to his room. Later on, he showed me his face. His lip was busted open. He explained what happened. That's all true and he wasn't a fighter at all," Diane shared.

"He's laughing now. He's saying that you were more freaked out that night than he was!"

"Yes, that's true," Diane agreed, her eyes widening. "No-one likes to see their child in a fight."

"He remembers that you used to get out and have a dance in the early days. He'd love for you to have some fun again. Even if it's playing music at home. Turn up the volume and dance like no-one's watching!"

We both started to laugh. She knew he was trying to encourage her to live life to the full.

"You're a little tense," I observed gently. "Just relax with me," I encouraged her.

Diane took a big breath. "Yes," she admitted softly.

"I understand there might be certain pieces of information you want him to say, but he's enjoying having a chat here. I think he's doing great so far."

"Yes, he is," Diane agreed. "I can feel him, I know he's here."

"He's laughing now, telling me that he's going to sit on your knee," I grinned.

Diane started to laugh.

"Actually, I feel he remembers doing that as a joke with you. He was like a big kid." I could feel very strongly that he was trying to help his mum relax during the reading.

"He must have been early twenties when he died?" I observed.

"Yes, twenty-two."

"He's taking me now to his last memories. He

was involved in a car accident, Diane. I can see the image of a country road. There was a bend on the road. It was night time. He's saying he lost control. When the car went over, it hit some trees and landed in a ditch. Does that make sense?"

Lifting her hands to her face, she began to weep. Calvin had been trying to ease his mum into the reading, but she had needed more validation. He kept on proving his presence with us by giving her more memories.

"I can feel now his passion for cars," I went on. "He's talking about mechanics in particular. Even when he was younger, he would have taken bicycles apart to see how the components worked. He had that interest as a boy; trying to add more speed or make the bicycle look more impressive."

"Yes," Diane responded quietly.

"I feel that was the beginning of his interest in cars and mechanics. He brings me to memories of his bedroom. He had posters of flashy cars. No women, pop stars or football teams on the wall; just cars," I told her smiling.

"Yes, that's true!" Diane remembered.

"He's showing me the 'Autotrader' now. He used to keep weekly copies, almost as though it was a book collection."

"Yes, my partner Joe used to give it to him every week. He would hold on to it. That's absolutely right," Diane agreed.

"I know he loved looking at images of cars. He didn't have a car at the time – he was too young to drive, but he kept visualising one. He remembers showing you the pictures and telling you about all the different models. Not that you had too much interest Diane, but he did," I laughed.

"That's so true, yes definitely," Diane chuckled.

"He loved that collection. It's still in his room today. He wonders do you know this?"

"Yes, they are," Diane nodded.

"Had he have lived; he would have gone on to work as a mechanic and have his own business. That was his potential," I shared. I could feel strongly Calvin's passion for anything related to the car industry. "He took pride in his car. Every day he would make sure it was cleaned properly; hoovering it, waxing it, making it shine. It had to be immaculate."

"Yes, that's him, he was studying at the time in mechanics when he died, he only had one week to go before his final exam, he loved cars,"

Diane shared emotionally.

"He's making me laugh now," I told her. "He's saying he mightn't have been immaculately groomed, but his car was! If anyone set anything down in his car, he would shout at them. He was so fussy and particular about his vehicle."

We were both chuckling at this vision of a scolding Calvin.

"That's so true," Diane grinned, amused.

"He was obsessed about his car," I said. "It was definitely his pride and joy."

"He remembers when he was fifteen, he used to work in a carwash for a family friend. He didn't work there for long, but it was a bit of extra pocket money."

"Oh wow, I had forgotten all about that! He did used to work in a carwash for a guy we knew. He was fifteen at the time," Diane confirmed.

"He's doing brilliant here; his character, hobbies, interests. His career aspirations, his love of cars. Not to mention the personal memoires between you both!" I was impressed by how much information Calvin was relaying to his mother.

"Yes, huge!" Diane agreed, nodding profusely.

"He remembers there was a place that used to race cars on a Sunday morning. It was like a rally. He used to go there with his friends. I don't feel he went there every week, but I can sense the track was up in the mountain. He loved the speed, the cars, the whole atmosphere. It was right up his street. Does that make sense?"

"Yes, one hundred per cent. I know where he's talking about," Diane validated.

"He's bringing me to other thoughts now, about his passing. He says he's sorry for leaving you so young. He knows he hasn't done anything wrong, but he knows the impact his death has had on everyone in the family. The devastation. He knows you feel empty without him, even though you have so many close family members. He has so much compassion and love for you all."

"Calvin is bringing me now to his romantic life," I observed, noticing a shift in his communication.

"I don't feel he brought too many girls home. I know he was a young guy, but he wasn't a typical bloke like other guys his age. He treated girls with respect. He would have gotten to know girls as friends first. He certainly didn't want to use anyone. Before he passed, he was talking to a girl he liked, but she wasn't his girlfriend."

"Yes, that's right, he didn't bring too many girls home, but he was popular with the ladies," Diane recalled.

"He's so easy-going Diane, so chilled-out," I laughed as I witnessed his attitude. "He knows there were a few girls fighting over him at the funeral. I think they hoped he was more than just a friend, but that wasn't the case."

Smiling, Diane agreed: "Yes, a few girls did argue over him. They all wanted a piece of him!"

"You know, he's proud of you for the way you're handling his death. For a while there, you thought you were sinking emotionally. It was almost like you felt you couldn't breathe, but you're doing your best now and taking each day as it comes."

Diane nodded in agreement. I could sense Diane was a spiritual person. She wanted to seek a spiritual solution to her problems.

"He's bringing a lovely memory of his baby days. He remembers you tickling him around the earlobes. He loved you doing that; it soothed him."

Diane smiled, reminiscing about his younger years. "Oh yes, that's right. I had forgotten about that."

"He knows you'll never fully accept his passing, but he's trying to soothe your anxiety. He knows you had some bad days recently; not getting out of bed, thoughts of wanting to join him, but you can feel his strength. He will keep you strong Diane. Thankfully, you have other children. They give you purpose. They need their mum. He's saying, 'I'm still here beside you too, you know'.

Diane opened up: "Yes, I feel him around me all the time."

"I feel he was complaining about a sore tooth before he passed," I said, becoming aware I was rubbing my tongue up around my teeth. I could almost feel his tooth ache.

"He's saying, 'Tell my mummy I got my tooth fixed.' Do you know if he needed a filling?"

"Yes, he did!" Diane exclaimed, surprised by this piece of information.

"That day of his passing, his face was swollen and red," Diane explained. "His toothache was annoying him and he was in pain. He had only eaten half a sandwich that day. It put him off eating."

"Well, his tooth is fixed now. He's no longer in any pain," I said, smiling at this wonderful piece of evidence for his mum.

"He wants you to rest, to nurture and care for yourself. You've been through so much. Now isn't the time for big changes, just allow yourself to be," I told her. "He's saying, 'Life is for living. You've got to get out and enjoy it. He wants you to know that it wasn't as frightening when he passed as you think."

"You will never, ever be without your son," I told her. "He will always be your guardian angel. He'll continue to support and love you. He knows you can't get over the shock of his passing, but he keeps saying, 'Mum, I'm okay, I'm okay'."

Tears fell down Diane's cheeks. The relief of hearing that he was okay overwhelmed her with emotion.

"Even though I may be here on my own without the family, I was still comforted by people I know in Spirit. They came for me," he shared to Diane.

"You have images in your mind about the accident, but he wants you to know he never suffered. He's giving you a massive hug and kiss. He's strong."

"Yes, so strong," Diane whispered.

"You must sit in his bedroom sometimes," I

observed. "He's showing me that you find solace and peace there. You talk out loud to him. Sometimes you lie on his bed. He is close to you there. He sees that you always end up crying for him in that room."

"He's messing about again now," I add. "He's saying, 'Mum, don't go there if it makes you feel that way. It will only make you feel worse, not better. Don't go in there, it's the room of doom!'"

Suppressing our giggles, we both smiled at his expression; 'the room of doom'.

"I feel he's trying to cheer you up; to keep you light-hearted. He's saying, 'I had a brilliant life and continue to do so even after death!' I still get to come around you all. You still feel my presence," I expressed Calvin thoughts.

"Yes, that's true," Diane agreed.

"Well, he's saying, 'If you're still feeling me, then where do you think I am? I'm happy, I'm good, I'm relaxed. He knows he'll be missed until you reunite again, but life is for living. He wants you to live your life joyfully in his memory."

I could feel Calvin's soul beginning to wane and the power around me fade; I knew the reading was coming to a close.

"I hope you take comfort from the experience,

Diane. Know that he will always remain with you, from Spirit side of life," I said, closing the reading. "He's finishing with saying 'My heart belongs to you, always'. He loves you so much." With those finishing words, I ended the reading.

"It's wonderful to know that the greater part of his soul is with me always. I won't fear death now. I'll still grieve for him, but I'll know he exists around me. My faith has been restored." Diane validated after the experience.

That's the Miracle of Mediumship. It rebuilds people's lives, comforts their mind and changes their perspective. It opens people's hearts, allowing them to love. It heals and comforts those dealing with loss. It transforms attitudes and belief systems. It paves a way of light. There is hope. You will have an eternal bond with every person you have ever loved. Their presence will never leave your side.

CHAPTER TWENTY-TWO

My Precious Angel

"TWINKLE, TWINKLE, LITTLE star, how I wonder what you are. Up above the world so high, like a diamond in the sky. Twinkle, twinkle, little star, how I wonder what you are."

Dawn sang lovingly to daughter Kendal as she bathed her. Little Kendal was born with no ears, but fortunately, she could pick out some sounds with the help of her specialised hearing aids.

As Kendal splashed around in the water listening to her mum singing, she tried to join in. Dawn smiled, appreciating the moment. Kendal was such a loving, caring child. A determined soul, she loved her mother, granny and family very much. Because of her hearing issues, she had learned sign language. She would constantly gesture the "thank you" sign to her mum.

Looking at her daughter in the bath, Dawn's mind flashed back to the first time she saw her baby girl on the hospital screen. The twenty-week scan should have been an exciting time for Dawn, but the look of concern on the doctor's face filled her with fear. This became the first of many trips to hospitals; journeying back and forth between various specialists and consultants.

When the doctors scanned Kendal, they couldn't find her heart chambers. Thinking it could just be the way the baby was positioned, they tried to reassure Dawn. However, instinctively, mum-to-be knew that something was seriously wrong.

At Dawn's twenty-three-week stage, she was called back for another scan. It was during this appointment that the Specialist revealed some very distressing news. Kendal was diagnosed with Hypoplasia, or what is known as 'Left Heart Syndrome'. Only the right side of Kendal's heart was working. This would affect not only most of her organs, but her lifelong chances of survival. Naturally Dawn was devasted, but being the strong mother that she was, she was determined to stay optimistic for her sake of her baby.

She wasn't so hopeful with her romantic relationship however. It had taken a turn for the worse during the pregnancy. Sadly, Dawn had discovered her partner's lies and infidelities. It was a crushing blow. Tired of his behaviour, she tried to be brave and decided to go it alone. She would gather all her innermost strength and move on from his abusive behaviour. With three children at home and one on the way, being a single parent was going to be tough.

Thankfully, her mum Amelia was on hand to help her cope with the stress. What they didn't realise however, was just how much stress they were about to go through.

Ten days after Dawn gave birth, Kendal had open heart surgery. She was given only a twenty per cent chance of survival. Against all odds, Kendal made it through the operation and survived. It was a terrifying time for everyone but Dawn could see her tiny spirit fighting to live.

At four months old, doctors experimented with hearing aids for Kendal. There were holes in place of where her ears should be and doctors were able to insert specialist hearing aids. For the first time ever, Kendal could hear her mum's voice.

"Kendal...Kendal... can you hear me? It's mummy. Hello baby."

Swinging her head in the direction of Dawn's

voice, Kendal's eyes lit up with pleasure. She could hear! It was an overwhelming emotional moment for everyone.

Due to the nature of her fragile condition, Kendal's health was monitored closely at all times. At only six months old, she had to go back into hospital for yet another open-heart surgery. Even after the operation was completed successfully, Kendal still had to be kept in hospital for several months to recover. Mum never left her side, patiently hoping for the day she would be able to bring her back home.

Little Kendal had tubes attached to her tiny body. Life-giving food and fluids were fed through the tubes, but often caused severe reflux. Doctors taught Dawn how to administer food and medication to Kendal, in preparation of getting her home from hospital.

Dawn was fully committed to Kendal's care; visiting the hospital daily as well as juggling her other children's needs. There was grocery shopping, clothes washing and housework, not to mention helping with homework. With the lack of any help from a partner, it was a stressful time for Dawn. Thankfully, Dawn's mum was an absolute blessing, helping out in whatever way she could.

At ten months old, Kendal was finally allowed to leave hospital and return home. It was a huge turning point for Dawn. With Christmas only a few weeks away, all the family would be together again. Normality could resume.

For the first few months at home, Kendal's health was gradually improving. Her older siblings doted on her, especially Mia who was only a few years older. Everyone spoiled her, lavishing love and attention on their little sister.

Kendal's upbeat attitude was inspiring. No matter what pain she was going through, there was a determination and fire from within which pulled her through. Despite all the odds, she was alive and thriving.

At eighteen months old, Dawn noticed Kendal's face and body appeared swollen. Panicking, she immediately took her to hospital, however the doctors didn't seem unduly concerned. Dawn's instinctive motherly instinct told her otherwise. Dismissing their initial advice, she pleaded with them to investigate further. Finally giving into her demands, they carried out more tests. It was then discovered that Kendal had developed 'nephrotic syndrome', meaning that her kidneys were damaged, hence the bloating.

It was a fatal condition that required immediate action. Kendal was given chemotherapy every six months to treat the illness. Alongside this, she also needed dialysis. It was an extremely worrying and fretful time. Mum sat devotedly at Kendal's hospital bedside from morning till night.

Kendal lost her beautiful auburn coloured hair, but kept her smile. Her strength and determination gave the rest of the family the ability to stay positive. For the next few years, they pulled together as a family and learned how to incorporate Kendal's condition into their everyday life. Dawn became Kendal's full-time carer, although everyone chipped in to help.

A real 'girlie-girl', Kendal loved dressing up. Mum always clothed her in cute pink dresses and put a little sparkly hairband over her head, covering her hearing aids. Gradually, her beautiful auburn hair began to grow back again.

Kendal and Mia loved 'Frozen'; the children's animation film with catchy songs. The sisters would sing along to their heart's content, watching it on repeat. They would play together happily, keeping each other company and making up their own fun.

They also couldn't wait for big sister Alesha to

have her new baby boy. She was weeks away from her birth and everyone was so excited about the new arrival.

At five years of age, Kendal was still having ongoing treatment. Dawn was used to this by now. She had settled in to a daily routine involving administering medication and changing Kendal's tubes and nappies. Because of her kidney problem, part of this regime was to check how much protein was in her urine.

One morning, Dawn noticed that the protein levels were unusually high. She decided to keep an eye on it over the next few days, however the situation didn't change. Concerned, she rang the hospital and explained the problem. She was put through to a doctor who didn't normally have Kendal as his patient. He advised Dawn to administer 40ml of steroids rather than the usual 30mls. Dutifully, Dawn followed his suggestion.

That evening, Kendal went to bed as normal. Walking up the stairs, she made her way into her big brother's room first.

Unable to pronounce his name 'Callum' yet, she called: "Night, night Calm."

Then, heading into her mum's bedroom, she climbed into bed.

"Night, night mummy. Love you," Kendal said, giving Dawn her normal night-time hugs and kisses.

Unsettled about the protein levels, Dawn knew something wasn't right. When she awoke to a choking sound, she knew it was Kendal. Rushing to her side, she could see that she was being sick. Frantic, Dawn rang 999 for an ambulance. It took them over an hour to arrive. When they finally turned up, they took Kendal's blood pressure and were alarmed by how low it had fallen. They told Dawn they might have to drill a hole in her leg.

Kendal was unresponsive. She wasn't opening her eyes and her complexion was pale. With Dawn by her side, Kendal was rushed to hospital in the ambulance. A team of around fifteen doctors were on hand, awaiting her arrival and ready to help. Kendal had to be resuscitated. When she became alert, she began crying out for her mummy. Dawn ran to her. She was never going to leave her side, ever.

The doctors decided to give Kendal a CT scan and it was Dawn's job to hold her down. As the specialists examined the results, Dawn could tell by the look on their faces that it wasn't good.

They asked for the scan to be done again. Dawn had no idea what was going on but she could feel the foreboding atmosphere. Kendal was then rushed from the CT room to Intensive Care. All Dawn could do was wait fretfully in the family room. It would be another four hours before the family got to see her.

When Dawn was called into the doctor's office, her stomach flipped. Thinking the worst, she was faced with the neurologist, the heart doctor and a few other specialists.

They confirmed her worst fears.

"Your daughter has suffered a right-handed cerebral palsy stroke. We need to carry out an immediate operation on her, but we have to tell you, we have never operated on a child before with this condition; only with adults. I'm very sorry to tell you, but there's a high risk that she could die on the operating table."

Stunned, Dawn sat there, her mouth open, listening to this devastating news. She couldn't absorb what she was hearing.

"I know this is difficult," the specialist explained, "But we need a decision within an hour. She is so sick that we have to move quickly. We'll need your permission as to whether you'll allow us to go ahead with the operation or not."

A sick feeling of dread sank into the pit of Dawn's stomach. How could she make a decision like that? Overwhelmed with the enormity of their request, she burst into tears, sobbing into the arms of her mother and her kids.

Right on time, the doctors returned within the hour, pressing for a decision.

"I can't," Dawn shook her head fiercely. "I can't do it. I can't take that risk. If my daughter dies on the operating table, she'll have no around her. If I take her home, at least we'll get a few more days with her."

"I'm very sorry," the doctor explained. "But we're going to have to put her into an induced coma. Do you want to give her a kiss before we do that?"

He didn't need to ask twice! Dawn leapt up and stared at her beautiful baby girl. Tears welled in the corner of her eyes, but she tried to stay strong. As soon as they wheeled Kendal away, Dawn broke down crying.

"The reason we're putting her into a coma," the doctor explained, "is to help her brain to rest. We can then try to take her out of it in a day or two to see how she reacts."

When they did try to take her out of the coma, she became irritated and agitated. The doctors had to sedate her again, breathing life into her via the ventilation machine.

When the doctor was doing his routine rounds on the ward, he noticed Kendal kick her leg. Not wanting to get her hopes up, Dawn could hardly believe it. However, when the doctor touched Kendal's leg, she pushed against him.

"Oh my God! My little girl is coming back!" Dawn rejoiced, hope soaring through her heart.

However, the joy was to be short lived. The following day, doctors decided to do another CT scan and the results weren't positive.

They could see from the scan that the stroke had spread to the base of the brain – the central area which had been keeping Kendal alive. Kendal was gradually fading away.

As Dawn and the family sat around Kendal's bed, they watched her heart monitor. The constant bleeps were now quietly decreasing. Dawn knew that her baby girl was dying.

In that moment, Dawn realised that her little girl's life was only being prolonged by a machine. Hadn't she had suffered enough? Two heart transplants, cancer, dialysis treatment and now strokes. No-one deserved this amount of pain.

"Stop it! Just stop all of it!" she exclaimed, sobbing uncontrollably. "She's had enough. She's only five years old. She can't take all this pain!"

The hospital specialists had to call a formal meeting with Dawn. They had to be one-hundred percent sure that Dawn wanted to stop Kendal's treatment. It was excruciating for Dawn. On the one hand, she wanted to beg them to save her, but on the other hand, she knew that nothing else could be done.

Dawn gave permission for the treatment to end. Kendal's life support machine would be turned off.

This was never the ending she wanted for her child. However, she made the decision with the deepest love and compassion. As a devoted carer and mother, she knew it was the right choice for Kendal.

Running from the doctor's room, Dawn rushed to Kendal's bedside. Crying uncontrollably, she climbed up next to her on the hospital bed. Curling behind her and holding her baby close, she covered her with hugs and kisses.

Wiping the tears from her face, she whispered: "I don't want you to go baby girl. Mummy loves

THE MIRACLE OF MEDIUMSHIP

you so much. But now it's time to stop fighting. It's time to go and be with the Angels." Dawn broke down crying once more, clutching her daughter close to her chest.

The medical staff arrived in the room, ready to start the process of removing the ventilation. Dawn couldn't watch. It was too devastating. Instead, her granny Amelia and Dawn's friend Heather, sat by Kendal's side while they slowly took out the ventilator.

Dawn was waiting downstairs, pacing back and forth.

Amelia ran downstairs to see Dawn. "You'll have to come up. She's waiting for you. She's holding on for her mummy. Her heart rate has risen. She wants you there, Dawn."

Dawn dashed back upstairs, bursting through the doors. Doctors and nurses were standing around the bed. The room had been prepared with dimmed lights. Gentle music played in the background. They had picked songs from Kendal's favourite movie 'Frozen'.

"Has she gone?" Dawn breathed, as she rushed over to Kendal's side.

"No, she's waiting for you. She's fighting it, holding on to say goodbye," the doctor replied softly.

Dawn lay her head gently on Kendal's chest. She could hear her soft heartbeat, feel her chest moving slowly up and down. Dawn climbed into bed beside her, put her arm under Kendal's head and pulled her close. She lifted her little legs over her body and held her. Kissing her face and lavishing her with mothering energy, she sat with Kendal in her final hour. After just a few minutes, Kendal took her last breath. Her beautiful angel made the transition to Spirit.

For the next few hours Dawn lay next to Kendal on the hospital bed. Singing her favourite songs softly to her, she held her close. "Twinkle, twinkle, little star". Dawn needed these precious few final hours to be alone with her daughter. Her courageous daughter who had overcome so much in her five years.

On 28th April 2020, Kendal gained her angel wings.

The funeral was beautiful. A horse and carriage carried her pink coffin. Hundreds of mourners came to show their support. Naturally, the family were heartbroken, but the impact on Dawn and granny Amelia was particularly hard.

Distraught, Dawn needed to know if Kendal was okay. Her desire led her to attend my medium night on Zoom. During lockdown, I still wanted to demonstrate for others, so I had decided to set up a few online events.

There were around thirty participants on screen. I don't normally work with angel cards, but on this particular evening, I felt drawn to. Pulling a card, I wanted to share it with one of the audience members.

"Can I come to you please?" I asked.

It was Dawn on the screen, although we had never met before. She seemed shocked I had picked her out.

"I have an Angel card here I want to show you."

I lifted the card up to the screen for everyone to see. The image was an Angel holding a little girl's hand.

"I feel you've lost a daughter, that's why this card is significant to you, does that make sense?"

Dawn burst into tears and couldn't speak. She raised her hand up to show five fingers. "Yes, just five weeks ago," she sobbed.

Everyone was taken aback by this connection. An overwhelming feeling of compassion poured from me towards Dawn.

"I have to be honest; I don't feel she's fully

ready to communicate yet. Maybe we can arrange a one-to-one appointment in a few months and try then," I advised, knowing that the right time would come.

Kendal's soul did return to communicate again with us.

It was June 2021. Lockdown had lifted and I was doing my demonstrations publicly again. I had seen hundreds of clients in between and I couldn't remember Dawn from the brief encounter on zoom. However, I noticed two women sitting in the audience together; a mother and daughter. I could feel a child with them so I invited them both onto the stage.

Sometimes people bring objects to my events; items that belong to loved ones passed. When I hold the object in my hand, it can help me to feel the essence and soul of the loved one I'm communicating with. I can see and feel their memories.

Dawn handed me a blanket and as soon as I touched it, I started swaying on my feet, rocking from side to side. I felt like I was holding a child in my arms.

"Your daughter is here," I began.

"I feel she was smaller than children of her

age. There were concerns about her growth. I can see trips back and forth from hospital, medical appointments at the doctors. It was going on for years, not just the last stages of her life. I feel that when she was born, there were already complications. Her health problems didn't develop until later, but during your pregnancy you knew there would be a difficult time ahead. Does that all make sense?" I asked.

"Yes, yes," Dawn nodded.

I kept rocking with the blanket, feeling her daughter's soul communicating through me. Looking at Dawn, I continued: "As a mother, you were determined. You kept thinking, 'I don't care what she has or what long-name-you-label-her as having. I'm her mummy. I'll do everything in my power to help her. She's my wee Angel.' Actually, you see your daughter as your Angel and I want to agree with you. That is her role to you from Spirit." I could feel the struggles the family had to go through, the strength they had to muster.

Dawn and her mum were nodding in agreement with everything I said.

I allowed the information to flow. "You haven't just come through the loss of your daughter, there have been other disappointments in your life. Can I share everything? It might get a little personal?"

"Yes, go for it," Dawn consented.

"Your daughter is bringing up the memory of her dad. You haven't always been supported by him. There was a really difficult period and she remembers you as a single parent. You raised her on your own without him, even from birth."

"Yes, I was always on my own," Dawn confirmed.

"She's saying, 'I know you had that disappointment but you were always there for me.' She knows that your mother helped you through the stressful periods."

"Even during those last periods of her life, it was hard to accept what was happening. She's showing me she had to get tests but you didn't want to believe the results. You kept asking the doctors to do them again. You didn't want to believe what they were telling you. Your mum and family were all there to help. You became protective and had to stand up for her. The doctors knew she was dying but as a mother you were searching for a way for her to live. It was so difficult to accept their news," I told her.

Dawn kept nodding in agreement.

"As she stands with me, I can hear her singing, 'Twinkle, twinkle, little star.'" I sang the nursery rhyme out loud.

"Oh my god!" Dawn gasped, lifting her hand to her open mouth.

I continued singing, adding in a line her daughter was telling me. "'Twinkle, twinkle, little star, how I wonder where you are. My mummy sang this to me every night."

Both of them were now crying. "Yes, I sang it every night at bath time," Dawn sobbed.

"Even when she was dying, she says you were holding her in your arms, rocking her back and forth. She was in the hospital bed, you were lying down next to her, comforting her. You looked at her beautiful face and long eyelashes that everyone used to comment on," I smiled. "She is saying, 'My mummy held me, singing.' You knew in that moment, that her time on earth was coming to an end. That feeling of powerlessness, the helplessness of not being able to save her, was overwhelming."

"Yes, that's why I tried to make every day special," Dawn replied, her eyes brimming with tears.

"She's so beautiful. She saying excitedly:

'Mummy, I can talk, eat, run. Walk, dance, sing!' She is fully energised now. There were a few disabilities that were holding her back in life, but she wants you to know that in Spirit, she's beyond those barriers. She's saying to you, 'I'm free'."

Dawn's shoulders heaved a sigh of relief.

"She no longer has any disabilities or restrictions," I reassured her.

Turning my attention now to her looks, I observed, "I feel she had ginger or auburn coloured hair."

"Yes, she did," Dawn agreed. "We all have that hair colour; it runs in our family."

"She's saying you cut two pieces of her hair. You kept two long curls."

Stunned, Dawn looked at her mum. Both of them nodded in agreement.

"You kept those curls," I repeated.

"Yes, one's in my mum's locket," Dawn told us.

"She's saying, 'I'm okay. I'm safe. She has met up her grandad and granny – that's your parents," I said, looking at Dawn's mum.

Amelia nodded in understanding.

"They are on either side of her, holding her

hands. They're looking after her in Spirit. You've prayed to your parents to be with her, and they want to let you know they have her safe."

Amelia agreed she had been saying those prayers.

"She's actually buried in the same grave as her granny and granddad," Dawn told us.

I motioned to my waist, copying Kendal's movements. "She's saying, 'I've filled out. I've no more weight problems."

"Yes, she lost loads of weight before she died," Dawn confirmed.

Smiling, I went on: "She's saying, when you think of her, think of her as having fun, dancing, singing. I feel she couldn't speak, and that's why she's so happy in Spirit."

"Yes, she had no ears," Dawn said.

I began dancing gently from side to side.

"Although she had hearing problems, I still feel she had her own made-up noises and words to songs. She was always singing and dancing. You always encouraged her to try to make sense of what she was hearing." I could feel how much she loved music and the joy in her soul as she connected with me.

"Please know, there's no illness or disability in

Spirit. Everything is normal again. With her and any soul," I reassured them.

"She knows you go to the ocean to find peace. You talk to her every day, but she feels that there's a special place where you can really connect with her. It's near the water. You can relax easier when you're there. She says she's with you when you are there, but she's with you all the time. Does that make sense?"

"Yes, it does," Dawn nodded.

"She was like a little princess. You had her dressed up in the prettiest outfits. She loved it though, she loved the style," I smiled, recounting this little diva's memories.

"She's singing, 'My mummy is the best mummy'. She's blowing raspberries, trying to make everyone feel jealous!' We all laughed as she teased the audience. 'I had the best mummy'."

"And I had the best daughter," Dawn shared back, overcome with emotion.

"I know you did," I agreed. "She is so beautiful, inside and out." I sighed, taking in the magnitude of the connection.

"I hope the biggest comfort you take from this, is that she has no more disability. She is free from all pain. For such a young child, she endured a lot. It was a constant battle; one health problem after another."

Dawn nodded and began to rattle off the list of complaints: "Chemo, open heart surgeries…"

"But in the end, the family were all together for her, around the clock. Supporting her and supporting you. She knows you were expecting her passing."

"Yes, we all knew she was going to die," Dawn admitted. "We had to turn the ventilator off. My mum was there when the doctors switched off the machine. But at the end we were both there."

"She's saying you did the right thing; for her, for her soul. She was never going to fill that vision that you hoped for your daughter. You've both gained an angel who watches over you twenty-four, seven. And I mean that, she will never leave your side."

As the reading came to a close, I asked in my mind, 'Is there anything else you want to share?'

As the thought went out, I lifted my hand to under my chin and scooped it outwards.

"That's her sign language," Dawn told me, tears choking her. "That's sign for thank you. She did that all the time."

I lifted my hand towards my mouth and blew a huge kiss.

A kiss to Dawn and granny Amelia from their beautiful Angel daughter, Kendal.

CHAPTER TWENTY-THREE
Spirit Signs

"I'M HOPING TO connect with someone special today. We have a secret code that we made before she passed. If she gives it to me, I will know she is okay and that it's her."

Nervously laughing, I acknowledged the young woman's request. She had come into my shop *House of Healing*, giving only her first name for the booking. This was common practice for me; I only ever took first names when people booked in by telephone.

"Well, let's just trust the process and be open to whomever connects," I replied calmly, although admittedly I was feeling the pressure. *A secret password?* I wondered what it could be.

Putting the thought out of my head and closing my eyes, I took a few moments to open my awareness to the Spirit world.

"I have a lady here," I started. "She was an aunt of yours, although I feel she was more of a mother to you."

"Yes, that's right," she confirmed.

I began describing her aunt and relaying all the memories she shared. With every piece of information I gave forth, the young lady confirmed that it was the person she had hoped to hear from.

But I still hadn't received the secret password!

As the reading progressed, I kept putting out the thoughts:

"What's the code word between you both?"

Still nothing. Yet even more information came streaming into my mind about her life.

"I'm going to close my eyes again," I announced decidedly. "Sometimes it helps; just give me a moment."

I closed my eyes, listening intently. Staying completely quiet, I awaited a response.

"Bubbles!" I blurted out.

"Oh my God! YES!" she exclaimed, excitedly. "That's our code word!"

Thank God for that, I thought.

Although she was given many other pieces of evidence that day, this was the validation she needed. This was the spirit sign to give the proof of her aunt's soul.

When someone dies, their priority is the people closest to them. The soul is the essence that moves into Spirit. The soul retains all the memories of physical life. When I communicate with someone passed to Spirit, I am communicating with that essence. Souls are able to share memories to prove that their consciousness lives on, they communicate telepathically to me.

Over the years, many people have told me about their own experiences of receiving signs from Spirit. These people are not mediums; they are ordinary people from all walks of life. Some are even people who had no interest in mediumship at all. And some are people who already had faith that loved ones were trying to reach them.

Loved ones in Spirit occasionally reach out to family and friends. Their aim is to help bring awareness of their presence. I call these *Spirit Signs.*

It's a loving interaction of Spirit trying to communicate directly to those they love. Below, you will read some of these real-life stories from regular, everyday people that have shared their experiences with me.

Sinead

MY HUSBAND'S FATHER passed away a few years ago. About a month after he died, we went on holiday. On the first day, my three-year-old son jumped into the hotel pool. I didn't realise how deep it was and jumped in straight after him. I can't even swim but as a mother, my natural reaction was to jump in anyway.

Connaire, my three-year-old son, clung onto my neck and began dragging me down with him. We were both sinking. Panicking, I thought we were going to drown.

Whilst we were both underwater, I kept thinking that if I didn't get him off me, I wouldn't be able to save us. I managed to get my son off my neck and was able to get above the water. I grabbed Connaire from underneath me and passed him to a helpful man at the poolside. Thankfully, we both survived.

Around a year later, we were driving to the cinema when memories of that holiday suddenly came up in conversation.

"Oh yeah, I remember that holiday, that's when I saw grandad," Connaire announced.

My jaw dropped open at his comment. Although completely shocked, I tried to keep a calm exterior. "What do you mean you saw grandad?"

"When I jumped in the pool, I saw grandad," he answered simply.

"There's no doubt about it, I firmly believe his grandad was looking out for him on that fateful day".

Kerry

I WAS A complete daddy's girl, and when my dad passed, my heart broke.

Dad had been in hospital for around six weeks, and I visited him every single day. It got to the point where the nurses actually had to ask me to leave, but I didn't want to. During the last few weeks, I even stayed with him throughout the night.

We would reminisce about old times. An artist and painter, his clothes were always covered in paint. The strong scent of paint thinners would waft behind him.

"If anything ever happens to me, look to the sky," he said, holding my hand. My sister Dee was on his other side. "Look for the rainbows. I'll have my paintbrush with me and I'll paint one whenever you need me."

The night before he died, I noticed he was losing his energy. My gut instinct told me that he was going to start his journey soon and leave us. I didn't want him to be left alone so I stayed overnight at the hospital. Sitting by his bedside, I wanted to make sure I was there for him at his final hour.

Looking up at me, Dad said softly, "Kerry, look to the skies when you need me. Tell the grandkids I'll paint them rainbows."

"You better not break your promise Dad," I said, squeezing his hand and gently teasing him.

I spent all night on the chair next to him; holding his hand, stroking it, doing my best to offer him some comfort.

The following morning, we all sat around his bed; me, my sister Dee, and mum. It was so hard to watch him in pain; a feeling of complete powerlessness. I knew he was uncomfortable and I pleaded with the nurses for a syringe driver to give him some relief.

He passed at 6.06pm that evening – 12th July 2016.

I was inconsolable. I think I actually lost a sense of reality. It was all a complete blur.

When we stepped outside the hospital, Dee

said, "Look up, Kerry."

My eyes were swollen and sore from crying, but as I looked up, I could see a faint rainbow. I wasn't satisfied by what I saw; I wasn't convinced it was distinct enough to be a sign.

On the car journey home, I kept looking up at the sky.

You broke your promise daddy.

He must have heard me because the sky cleared and two of the brightest, most beautiful rainbows appeared!

I was utterly overwhelmed and completely relieved. I knew it was a sign. Dad was telling us that he was safe.

Every time I see a rainbow or a beautifully coloured sky, I know my dad is telling me that all is well.

We buried dad with a paintbrush tucked in his chest pocket. Photos of his grandchildren were placed in his hands. He was the heart and soul of our family and I honestly didn't think I would ever survive the grief. However, being a mum to three children and a devoted partner to Neil, I had to keep going.

When Neil was thirty-one years old, he had been diagnosed with testicular cancer. Due to his chemo, we'd been given zero chance of having any more kids.

However, miracles do happen.

I fell pregnant during Neil's cancer treatment, giving birth to our beautiful daughter Amber.

A year after dad passed, I got pregnant again. This time with a baby boy – my only son. I named him 'Ivan' after my beloved dad. I believe it was a blessing from dad, and a blessing from God. I'm not an overly religious person but I do believe in God.

My son didn't get to meet dad, but he tells people that grandad paints rainbows in the sky for him.

Sometimes I get reminders of dad's presence. When I'm desperately missing him, somehow the smell of paint thinners lingers around me. The scent comforts me so much and helps to heal the pain in my heart. I swear I can hear his voice in my head.

"I'm okay. And you, my love, you will be okay too."

Kelly

I USED TO love watching the TV series 'Most

Haunted' with my mum. We enjoyed chatting about the paranormal and Spirits; a subject that fascinated both of us.

Mum was very open-minded to the Spirit-world and said she could sense the other side. She told me how she had seen her deceased mummy standing by her bed one night. This both terrified and intrigued me in equal measures!

My husband however, was the sceptic among us. When we went to visit mum, the conversation got around to the topic of afterlife.

"Spirit can't communicate!" he exclaimed. "It's all a load of nonsense."

Mum joked back with him. "Okay then, but when I die, I'm going to haunt you down!"

We laughed it all off at the time and I honestly never gave it a second thought.

Suffering from COPD, Mum's health started to deteriorate. Caring for her night and day, I stayed faithfully by her side, trying my best to comfort and support her.

When she was sleeping, I whispered in her ear: "Mummy, when you pass, can you give me a sign that you're okay, but please don't scare me."

Mum lost her battle with the illness shortly after this. She passed in January 2009.

Ringing my husband to share the sad news, he was crying uncontrollably.

"I knew it. She's been here. I felt an incredible wave of something move through me. I knew it was her!" he sobbed.

At 11.20am, the moment that mum died, he noticed that our three-month-old daughter began staring at one particular spot of the room. Initially wondering what she was looking at it, he just knew it was mum with them in the room. He felt it.

Mum was giving me the sign that she was okay. It frightened the life out of him, but it consoled me.

Laura

MY UNCLE PASSED on 17th October 2020. A post-mortem had to be carried out and his body was taken away the following day. With his remains gone, it seemed so quiet in his house without him. Along with my mum and my sisters, we decided to embark on the difficult and emotional task of tidying up his personal belongings.

We were all upstairs cleaning and I was clearing out a chest of drawers. I came across some old photographs. At that moment, I heard a very clear shout coming from the bottom of the stairs: "Laura!"

Startled, I ran to the top of the stairs to have a look, but I knew there was no-one downstairs.

I just knew it was my uncle calling me.

Lauren

WHEN I WAS only five months pregnant, I started experiencing physical pains that felt worryingly extreme. Alarmed, my partner and I decided to go to hospital to get checked out.

Lying on the hospital bed, the doctors had inserted a drip in my arm and asked me to keep it upright. I was kept in overnight for observation.

During the night, I had a very strong sense that my grandfather was close to me. He had passed away years before. The feeling stayed with me all night.

Sadly, my baby passed away.

My partner arrived the following morning, devastated to hear about the miscarriage. I insisted we name our son, Tommy, after my grandad.

There was no way I'd have him buried at the hospital. I vowed to have him laid to rest next to my grandparents.

Years later, I got the opportunity to visit a medium. Grandad confirmed that my son was with him in Spirit. When my arm was held aloft with the drip, my grandad was holding my hand the whole time. He reassured me that I had done the right thing burying my son with him and granny rather than at the hospital.

This gave me great peace.

Julie

I WENT TO a medium fifteen years ago. At the time she told me that my baby, who had sadly passed, wanted to connect. She wanted to show herself to me.

Terrified, I refused to accept her prediction and put it out of my mind.

"Mummy", I heard a voice behind me whisper. I was alone in my kitchen one evening, looking for something. "Mummy." I spun around but no-one was there.

My two girls were in bed so I knew it couldn't be either of them, but I walked into the living room to double-check. No sign. Going upstairs to their bedroom, they were both fast asleep.

I firmly believe my baby was trying to connect with me.

Natasha

I'VE ALWAYS ASSOCIATED robins with my granny. She loved robins and every time I spotted one, I took it as a sign she was there.

On one unfortunate day, my car broke down at a busy and dangerous junction. I just about managed to move it to a safe spot, but was crying my eyes out and having a panic attack. In my head, I heard the word: "Look."

I glanced to my left and a little robin was staring right back at me.

Immediately, a feeling of calm came over me. I just knew that everything was going to be okay. It helped me to focus until I got help.

I believe the robin was a sign from my granny that everything would work out, which in fact, it did!

Marita

HAVING JUST PASSED my driving test a few months beforehand, I was excited to be out on the road. Driving along a one-way road with two lanes, I had the option to use any lane.

"Get into the other lane." There was a little voice in the back of my mind but I ignored it.

"Get into the other lane," the voice persisted. Again, I ignored the voice and drove on.

"GET INTO THE OTHER LANE!" the voice shouted loudly in my head.

Finding myself speaking aloud and switching to the left lane, I exclaimed: "Okay!"

My friend in the passenger seat glanced at me sideways, giving me a strange look.

"Who are you talking to?" she asked.

I didn't have time to answer. A vehicle unexpectedly pulled out of nowhere almost hitting my car. They swerved into the lane I would have been in. If I hadn't switched lanes at that precise moment, there would have been an almighty crash. From then on, I always listen to that voice.

That 'voice' saved us.

Patricia

I'VE ALWAYS 'SEEN' Spirit when someone in my extended family dies.

At 8.30am one morning, I was walking to work with my husband when I saw a dark figure run towards a wall.

I was holding my husband's arm at the time and he saw it too. Curious, we walked towards the wall, examining it. There was no sign of anyone and the wall was too high and too thin for anyone to hide behind it.

Phoning my mum, I relayed to her what had just happened.

It was then that she told me they had just received a phone call. My aunt had passed away at 8.30am.

Catherine Louise

GRANDAD PASSED AWAY when I was thirteen. On the night he died, mum was up at the hospital while me and my brother stayed at nan's. It was bonfire night and fireworks were exploding outside. The noise woke me and when I glanced at the clock, I noticed it was 12.10am.

Just at that moment, standing right beside my bed, was grandad. I started crying, unsure of what was happening. Lovingly, he told me not to cry. He asked me to look after my nan, and then he disappeared.

I rushed to tell my brother what I had just

seen. He dismissed the idea altogether, telling me not to wake Nan over something so silly. I was adamant; what I saw and heard was real. Mum arrived home in the early hours. She told us that grandad passed away at 12.05am.

Many years later, I had a similar experience. It was eleven days after I gave birth to my second son Mason. I awoke at 5am, feeling like my grandad was standing next to me, but I didn't see him this time. Feeling weak, tired and rather unwell, I just wanted to go back to sleep.

"Wake up Catherine," I heard him say. I could feel him pushing me, urging me to get up. I didn't want to, but a force propelled me out of bed. Walking to the end of the bed, I haemorrhaged with a retained placenta.

My partner dialled 999 immediately and an ambulance rushed me to hospital. Grandad stayed beside me the whole time. With him by my side, I stayed calm and peaceful despite all the chaos happening around me.

I lost consciousness for a short while but again, it was a peaceful experience. When I woke, the doctors told me I had been very lucky. They said that if I continued sleeping, I may not be here today. They explained that by getting out of bed and standing up, it removed the blockage and saved my life.

I spent three days in hospital and made a full recovery. I haven't seen or heard Grandad since, but I know that when I need him, he'll be there.

I like to think that the night he died, heaven lit the sky for him with fireworks.

Grandad is my guardian angel.

Lorraine

I WAS ONLY sixteen when my Daddy died. Mummy had died eighteen months before.

The extended family came to our house to prepare for Dad's wake. One of my aunts started bossing me around and telling me what to do.

"Clear off!" I told her, storming out of the house. It was a cold February night and I made the trek over to my teacher's house, who was also a family friend.

My teacher ushered me in out of the cold. It was cosy inside with a blazing fire roaring in the grate. Her dog, an Irish wolf hound named Aoife, was stretched out on the rug.

Crying, I told my teacher that Daddy had died. Interrupted by Aoife, she began barking and running to the other end of the room; her hairs standing on end.

"Hold on Lorraine, tell me in a minute," my teacher replied, flustered by the dog's reaction. "I need to let her out. There must be a cat or something."

She pulled back the curtains to open the patio doors. Aoife stopped barking and stood still, quiet as a mouse, staring at the doors. Puzzled by the dog's reaction, I looked at the patio doors, only to see my Daddy standing smiling at me.

Aoife turned away quietly and lay back down beside the fire.

Marie

"WRITE A THANK you card to Angela because she is going to connect with me in Spirit tomorrow night."

Those were the words of my late Dad, talking to me in a vivid dream.

I had planned to go to an Evening of Mediumship at Belfast Castle the following evening. Angela was the guest medium.

The dream woke me at 4am, so I decided to follow my father's instruction.

My hobby is calligraphy, so picking a blank card, I wrote a thank you note and placed it in my handbag.

At the group reading, Dad came through, loud and clear. Despite the sadness of losing him, it was such a lovely feeling to connect with him again.

At the end of evening, I went up to Angela and thanked her, taking the prepared card and handing it to her. She joked that I must be the psychic one because I knew he'd come through.

Patricia

"THAT MAN IS sticking his tongue out at me! It's not fair, he's tricking me!"

My daughter, Esme, only two and a half years old, had been playing in the garden of my granny's house.

Thinking it was just her imagination, I placated her and sent her back outside to play.

Ten minutes later, she came back in, even more determined.

"Mummy, that man! He's still doing it! And he's telling me to say hello to Granny Rosie!"

She then walked over to the table and pointed

to a framed photograph. It was a black and white photo of granny and grandad from the 1950's.

"Look! That's him!" she exclaimed.

My daughter had never met grandad.

Katie

AFTER MY DAD'S funeral, I went home and lay in bed. I felt someone come into my room so I looked up to see who it was, but no-one was there. Lying back down, I felt a hand touch my arm very gently. A very distinct scent hung in the air – it was Dad's after-shave. I have absolutely no doubt that it was my dad that day, checking in on me.

Maureen

SIX MONTHS AFTER my dad died, I received a heavenly phone call.

It was one morning; the telephone rang and I answered. No-one responded. At that moment, I felt an overwhelming sense of peace. I could hear music going through my mind. I was so happy – I knew it was my dad giving me a sign.

Geraldine

MY HUSBAND PASSED away six months ago. I can feel his arms around me as I sleep. It has happened a few times now and gives me great comfort.

Charlene

IT WAS COMING up to my nanny's third anniversary and we were all really struggling. I have two boys aged 9 and 4. My oldest and I were both having a little cry about the upcoming anniversary. We missed nanny so much. As the years were passing, we were afraid we might forget the sound of her voice. I didn't tell my mum about how upset we were – I knew she was struggling just as much as me.

Mum rang the next day in floods of tears. She said that she'd had a really vivid dream about nanny. In the dream she walked into her living room and nanny was sitting in her chair knitting; a blanket draped over her knee. The blanket was glowing vibrant white. Mum asked nanny: "What are you doing?"

Nanny replied "I'm knitting for the boys Logan and Leo. They're afraid they're forgetting me."

Nanny opened her hand and gave two bright white feathers to my mum.

Mum sobbed as she relayed the dream to me. The dream had felt so real.

I decided to call over to mum's house to make sure she was okay. Walking up the path, I noticed two white feathers were placed side by side at the front door. One was a little bigger than the other, as though made especially for my boys.

I know it was a sign from nanny.

Shelly

MY DADDY PASSED away when I was only fourteen. I was so upset that I couldn't bear to hear his name or talk about him. It was just too painful. I couldn't even bring myself to visit his grave.

Until one night, when I had a bizarre experience.

I saw my daddy in my room. I could hear him telling me that he was okay; that I shouldn't be worrying about him. He told me that he was better now and he'd be able to watch over me. I could smell him so distinctly and I could feel him hugging me.

That was a huge turning point for me. For the

first time in weeks, I was able to talk about him and to say his name. I've even been to the grave to visit him!

I've mentioned to some people about my experience but they've fobbed me off by saying, "Oh that was just a dream."

But I know it wasn't a dream. It was so real and vivid. I know daddy was with me that night, reassuring me.

Connie

MY LATE GRANNY and I were very close and I missed her dearly. One evening, when I was feeling low, I asked aloud: "Granny, if you're with me, please show me a sign."

That night, my husband woke me, asking: "What is that ball of light in our bedroom?"

A bouncing ball of light was moving around the ceiling!

"Oh, that's granny," I replied casually. "I asked her for a sign today."

"Don't be silly!" he retorted, getting out of bed and inspecting the room, wondering where the light was coming from.

Of course, he found nothing.

Getting back into bed, he lay beside me, watching the beautiful energy bounce around the ceiling. It lasted twenty minutes before suddenly disappeared.

"You're right," he admitted, looking over at me. "That was granny."

Maureen

AFTER MY HUSBAND passed, I visited his grave almost every day. In the graveyard one evening, the moon was shining brightly overhead. Three dark figures walked past, but it didn't frighten me. I knew it was my mum, dad and husband; I saw them clearly. A feeling of peacefulness came over me; I knew I wasn't alone in life.

Annemarie

MY MOTHER HAD died a few months before and I was missing her terribly. I was living in a flat with my new born baby and going through a lot of changes.

Joanna was fast asleep in her cot so I nipped out to the balcony for a quick cigarette. Weirdly, I heard Joanna's music box playing. Thinking she may have woken, I rushed into her room, only to find her sound asleep.

How did this toy start to play on its own? Maybe it was a sign from my mummy!

"Mummy, is this you playing with Joanna's toy?" I asked aloud.

The bedroom light flicked on and off.

Teresa

ON THE NIGHT my granny passed, I saw her standing at the bottom of my bed smiling at me. Mum got the news an hour later; granny had died of a massive heart attack.

Emma

AFTER MY WEE son died, I was feeling extremely low. Suddenly, the smell of him passed by me. It was the most amazing warm feeling. I just knew he was there.

✧   ✧   ✧

I HOPE YOU take some comfort from reading these true stories. They are everyday people, having their own amazing experiences from Spirit, without the need for a medium like myself.

Spirit wants to comfort us and let us know they are still present in our lives. They love us, even beyond death. That will never change. Our loved ones passed continue to care for us. They want to assist each of us in our everyday life.

They will prove their existence to you in their way, not *your way*. So many people are waiting for certain signs. Sometimes they make demands of *how* they want their sign. Spirit will never frighten; they will only give us what we can emotionally accept. Spirit signs help build faith. They impact people positively, restoring their belief that departed family and friends are consciously living on.

Like all the work I have witnessed over the years, Spirit's only wish is to improve our lives. If you receive a Spirit sign, it will uplift you. Spirit signs move beyond the rational mind. You will *know* you've had an experience. It will change you; your outlook on life, your awareness and your thoughts about the afterlife. Spirit authenticates their presence to you through personal evidence.

Spirit wants to awaken us Spiritually. You are loved unconditionally. There is a power so loving. It wants to remove all fear of death. It has a greater plan for each of you. Trusting in this power takes time. Be gentle with yourself, be patient with your demands. God's power is helping to reunite souls together.

May the Power of healing shine through your life to show you the truth. May your losses be transformed by renewed faith and positivity. May your days ahead be blessed with joy and uplift-ment. May you take the comfort that all feelings of loneliness will pass. May the Power of Spirit give you strength in every area of your life. God bless.

Spirit never leaves us. They never will. Their love to you is constantly streaming towards you, always. That's the Miracle of Mediumship.

About the Author

ANGELA CURRENTLY RESIDES at her home in Belfast, Northern Ireland. Her passion and love for her work continues today through teaching, private one-to-one readings and demonstrations. She lives with her daughter, Gabrielle, who, like her mum, has shown an inherited gift for healing and communicating with those passed to Spirit.

Angela uses her abilities to uplift individuals and help them to understand that death is an illusion. Those in Spirit continue to help us evolve.

#miracleofmediumship
Facebook: @angeladunlopmedium
Instagram: @angeladunlopmedium
Website: www.angeladunlop.co.uk